Covent
Garden

Covent Garden

Its Romance & History

REGINALD JACOBS

NONSUCH

Cover illustration: Robert Smirke's Theatre Royal, Covent Garden, from Bow Street. From Papworth's *Select Views of London* (1816), plate 28, page 61.

First published 1913
Copyright © in this edition Nonsuch Publishing, 2007

Nonsuch Publishing
Cirencester Road, Chalford, Stroud, Gloucestershire, GL6 8PE
www.nonsuch-publishing.com

Nonsuch Publishing is an imprint of NPI Media Group

British Library Cataloguing in Publication Data.
A catalogue record for this book is available from the British Library.

ISBN 978 1 84588 362 1

Typesetting and origination by NPI Media Group
Printed in Great Britain

Contents

Introduction to the Modern Edition   7

Preface   9

Chapter I   11

Chapter II   17

Chapter III   21

Chapter IV   31

Chapter V   41

Chapter VI   49

Chapter VII   59

Chapter VIII   73

Chapter IX   81

Chapter X   91

Chapter XI   103

Chapter XII   111

Chapter XIII   119

Chapter XIV   131

Appendix   137

Introduction to the Modern Edition

Covent Garden is today one of London's most popular tourist attractions. The square and its surrounding streets have developed into a busy centre for entertainment, brimming with shops, arts and crafts, theatres and street performers. For much of its existence, however, Covent Garden served as the largest fruit and vegetable market in England, until its eventual relocation in 1973. This move brought to an end its long history of agriculture and trading, which had characterised the area since the beginnings of a formal market-place first appeared in the seventeenth century.

However, Covent Garden's market-place links stretch back even further than this. The original plot of land was occupied throughout the middle ages by the convent of St Peter. Here, the monks maintained a large kitchen garden to provide them with daily food. This 'convent garden' became a major source of fruit and vegetables for the citizens of London, who purchased the surplus goods, and was managed by a succession of leases granted by the Abbot of Westminster. Henry VIII's Dissolution of the Monasteries led to all such land being appropriated by the Crown. It was then granted in perpetuity to John Russell, the first Earl of Bedford. This land-owning family gradually developed it into a residential area, and, by the seventeenth century, the potential for real property development was seized upon. Architect Inigo Jones was commissioned to build an Italian-influenced piazza square and a grid of streets surrounding it.

It was in 1644 that the first shop opened in the piazza, and in the subsequent decades a combination of factors contributed to the growth of further trade. The Great Plague saw the residents of the City of London flee the city walls to seek the surrounding open spaces. The Great Fire of London destroyed many businesses, forcing merchants to look elsewhere for new premises. Trade thus began to flourish around the piazza, and in 1670 the Earl of Bedford petitioned the King to formalise the market for the purposes of buying and selling fruit, vegetables and flowers. He obtained the grant that allowed him and his heirs forever to hold a market there, every day, except Sundays and Christmas Day. Over the next century the character of the Covent Garden area evolved, and with this the market prospered. The Restoration infused London with new gaiety, and the taverns, coffee houses and cockfighting pits of Covent Garden became its centre for entertainment. These changes, and the exodus of the upper classes wishing to escape the noise, dirt and bustle that accompanied them, gave the area a bohemian air, attracting artists, thespians and more market traders. With this came an increase in poverty, however, and the lack of sanitation saw epidemics of cholera in the decaying tenements.

The Bedford estate attempted to control these problems, initiating programmes of renewal and stricter controls on leases for new traders. It continued, also, to develop and improve the market area design. The building of the covered market was completed in 1830, with glass roofs added in 1875 and 1899; the home of the new foreign flower market, the Jubilee Hall, was completed in 1904. The four hundred years of sole ownership by the Bedfords ended in the early twentieth century, by which time it was becoming clear that the market was unsuitably located. Its relocation was periodically suggested, and finally took place in the 1960s. Plans to tear down the market buildings were fought by local residents, and the area was instead renovated, transforming it into the vibrant tourist attraction that it is today.

Preface

Where holy friars told their beads,
And nuns confess'd their evil deeds.
But, oh! sad change! Oh! shame to tell
How soon a prey to vice it fell.
How? since its justest appellation
Is grand Seraglio to the nation.

(*Satire*, 1756)

In presenting a history of "Covent Garden and its Immediate Neighbourhood," I am conscious of dealing with some subjects which have already engaged the attention of various writers; but the absorbing interest of these subjects and their intimate connection with Covent Garden must be my excuse for having sketched them in brief outline.

My object has been to present to the public a purely historical and topographical account of one of the most interesting spots in the metropolis, written in a brief and popular form, and therefore I have refrained from dealing at any length with its special business aspects. I have simply added a short account of the various fruits and vegetables which are regularly supplied in such enormous quantities to Covent Garden and make that market famous throughout the civilised world.

REGINALD JACOBS
1913

I

*Early history—Derivation of name—First owner—
Bedford House—Sir W. Cecil's lease—Letting out of the
property*

"Can these dry bones live?" was the question put to Ezekiel by the Spirit of God in a vision. And the prophet was bidden to prophesy upon them, and the "bones came together, and the sinews and the flesh came upon them, and the skin covered them above."

A similar task is set before any one who desires to revive the dead past of any locality; to clothe with flesh and blood its bony squares and streets, and to set them moving once more with the hum of life, the encounters of wits and statesmen, the busy throng of poets and critics, the full-flushed tide of blood that animated the scholars, the traders, the intriguing courtiers, and the many-headed mob, whose bones, now dry, once hustled and pushed and throve and elbowed their way to their own objects in the streets and squares that know them no more.

To realise such a vision completely would require the inspired eye of the prophet. To attempt it by means of the careful study of old authorities is the object of this book.

No one will deny that Covent Garden is one of the most interesting spots in the metropolis. It was once part of the open country between the City and the village of Charing. The neighbouring Abbey of Westminster acquired it, and its monks used it as a garden and burial-ground.

It was subsequently granted by the Crown to the Russell family, who improved the property to such an extent that it rapidly became notable not only as the haunt of fashion, but also as that of vice.

The first official notice of Covent Garden in any plan of London is in a map by Aggas published in the reign of Elizabeth. It there appears as a small oblong space enclosed by a brick wall, and bounded on the south by a highway, the Strand (then a small lane), and on the north by fields and meadows extending as far as the heights of Hampstead and Highgate. Maitland says it dates back from 1222, and Mr Hare ("Walks in London") says it was originally known as Frère Pye Garden. In the fifteenth and sixteenth centuries its appellation was Convent Garden, no doubt because of its use by the monks of Westminster. Mr Timms says that in 1632 it was called "coven" or "common" garden. The latter appellation is obviously one of those "translations" such as Bottom underwent; such as may be seen in the signs of inns all over the land, whereby the Bacchanals became the Bag-o'-nails, and the Boulogne Mouth was converted into the Bull and Mouth.

In a legal document of 9 Eliz. we find "some messuages with garden thereto …" called "the Convent Garden." Also, after the death of Francis, Earl of Bedford, it was found that he held "1 acras terre et pasture, cum. partinentiis vocat. the Convent Garden, jacentes in parochia S. Martini in campis juxta Charinge-Cross in Com. Midd. ac vii acras terre et pasture vocat. the Longe Acre adjacentes prope Convent Garden predicta." (A beautiful specimen of Monk-lawyer Latin, the perpetration of which by any fourth-form boy to-day would arouse in his headmaster a desire to correct his terminations.)

The earliest proof met with that Covent Garden belonged to the Abbey Church of Westminster is found in Malcolm's "Londinium Redivivum," 1803,[1] where it is stated that in 1539, when the possessions of the Church were being confiscated, that Abbey was compelled to accept lands belonging to the disestablished Priory of Hurley in exchange for its manor of Hyde and several others, including Covent Garden. The latter, close to London, was obviously more valuable than the former, but the monks, being no longer top-dog, had to "take it or leave it." Doubtless Henry VIII quoted the handy proverb, "Exchange is no robbery," and one doesn't argue with "the master of thirty legions," whose premiss is "Le Roy le Veult," and whose conclusion is the Block. That Covent Garden was used by the monks as a burial-ground appears likely from the fact that a number of bones were unearthed on this spot when the market was rebuilt in 1829.

After the dissolution of the monasteries the property of Covent Garden was given to Protector Somerset, on whose attainder and execution it reverted to the Crown. In 1552 it was bestowed by Letters Patent on John Russell, first Earl of Bedford, together with seven acres of land, now known as Long Acre. The Earl built his town residence on his newly acquired property on the site of the present Southampton Street. This edifice, constructed mostly of wood, existed till 1704, when, like other palatial mansions in the neighbourhood, in the course of time it was swept away. The gardens of Bedford House stretched northwards, the wall forming the southern boundary of the future market. The Bedford family had previously resided in the Bishop of Carlisle's Inn, very near the spot where their newly erected mansion rose.

In 1570 part of the estate was let to Sir William Cecil, afterwards the great Lord Burleigh. A copy of the lease appears in "Archæologia" (vol. xxx. p. 494) "of all that his porcyon or parcell of grounde lyenge in the east ende and being parcell of the enclosure or pasture commonly called Covent Garden, scituate in Westm, which porcyon the said Sir Willm Cecill doeth and of late yeares hath occupied at the sufferance of the said Earl and hath bene and now ys dyvyded from the rest of the said enclosure called Covent Garden on the west side of the said porcyon or p'cell nowe demysed with certaine stulpes and rayles of wood and is fensed with a wall of mudde or earth on the east next unto the comune highwaye that leadeth from Stronde to St Giles-in-the-Fields and on the west ende towards the south is fensed with the orchard wall of the said Sir Willm Cecill and on the south ende with a certaine fense wall of mudde or earth being therebye devyeded from certaine gardens belonginge to the Inne called the Whyte Harte[2] and other tenements scituate in the High Streete of Westm, commonly called the Stronde," etc.

Sir William Cecil's dwelling was situated in the High Street at the south end of Drury Lane on the site of the original parsonage of St Martin's-in-the-Fields. The house was originally built by Sir Thomas Palmer in the reign of Edward VI (Stow). It is not clear what use Cecil made of the portion of the estate; probably he made use of it for stabling purposes. That some shanties had been erected is certain, as Strype, in his description of the neighbourhood, writes: "The ground on which this parish was built was formerly fields with some thatched houses, stables and suchlike, which lying in so good a place, the owner of the said ground did think good to make an Improvement thereof, and procuring an act of Parliament for the making of it into a Parish of itself, disunited from St Martin's-in-the-Fields, did about the yeares 1634–5, begin to pull down the said old buildings, and clear away the rubbish, and laid it out in several fair streets, straight and uniform," etc.

The Cecils were evidently always keen on purchasing the property of Covent Garden from the Bedford family. On April 27, 1610, Edward, Earl of Bedford, wrote to the Earl of Salisbury that "He could not sell his inheritance of Covent Garden, having bound himself under a heavy penalty not to further impoverish himself by the sale of his property" (Cal. State Papers, 1603–4, p. 604).

In 1627 only two persons were rated to the parish of St Martin's-in-the-Fields under the head "Covent Garden."

Strype also mentions a lease from which it appears that the Earl let out portions of his property as follows:

"I find by a lease dated the 10th day of March 1631, in the seventh year of the reign of King Charles I, granted by Francis, Earl of Bedford, to John Powell of Little Thorocke, in the county of Essex, Clerk; and to Edward Palmer, of the parish of St Andrew's, Holborn, in the county of Middlesex, Gent., son of Edward Palmer, late citizen and Girdler of London, lately deceased; and John Borradaile of London, he having let unto the former Edward Palmer, the Father, all the piece or parcel of ground of the said Earl's pasture called Covent Garden and Long Acre; one of them lying on the south side of a parcel of ground then laid forth for a new churchyard, containeth in length, from a parcel of ground then preserved for a Vestry House; on the east, 180 feet and 3 inches of Assize, and in Breadth, from a parcel of ground then laid forth for a street, Way or Passage of 50 foot broad on the south side of the said piece of ground laid forth for the said churchyard on the North, 33 foot of assize, and all other Conveniences for Building, to hold for 34 years to come, from the date aforesaid at the yearly rent of seventeen pounds and six pence, payable Quarterly, at or in the Dining Hall of the said Earl's commonly called Bedford House in the Strond, of the parish of St Martin's-in-the-Fields."

Strype goes on to say that the above-mentioned Palmer (the elder) "did, at his own charge, erect nine several Messuages or Tenements on the said ground."

It is curious that this lease does not appear in any other account of the market. A perusal of the same makes it clear that plans had already been made by the Earl as to his future building operations; the lease bearing date 1631, and the church, market square, and piazzas having been constructed in 1633–8. The patent for the market was not granted till 1671. Thus it appears that from the time of the building of the church and the general improvements until the latter date, a great portion of the estate was let.

1. See Appendix.
2. See Appendix.

II

The first steps taken by the Earl of Bedford were to demolish the old shanties, and to clear the property of all such encumbrances. He then called in to his assistance the celebrated architect Inigo Jones, under whose instructions were built the Piazzas or Portico Walk, which will be described in another chapter, and also the fine mansions and Church of St Paul.

In 1668 the whole area of the square was gravelled and enclosed by rails, and in the middle a column surmounted by a sundial was erected.

Strype writes: "Within the rails is a stone Pillar or Column raised on a pedestal ascended by steps, on which is placed a curious Sun-Dial, four square, having above it a mound gilt with gold, all neatly wrought in Freestone."

With regard to this the following entries appear in the accounts of the Churchwardens of the Parish:

Dec. 7, 1668.— Received from the Rt. Honl. the Earle of Bedford, as a gratuity towards erecting of ye column, £20 0s. 0d.

Dec. 7, 1668.— Received from the Rt. Honl. Sir Charles Cotterell, Master of the Ceremonies, as a gift towards the said column, £10 0s. 0d.

Ap. 29, 1669.— Received from the Rt. Honl. The Lord Denzill

Holles, as a present towards the erecting of the column, £10 0s. 0d.

Nov. 27, 1668.— For drawing a modell of the column to be presented to the vestry, £0 10s. 0d.

Dec. 2, 1668.— To Mr Wainwright for 4 Gnomens, £0 8s. 6d.

The column existed for a considerable period, and was a favourite spot where old women congregated in order to sell milk, porridge, broth, etc.

The following lines appeared in 1738:

High in the midst of this most happy land
A well-built marble pyramid does stand;
By which spectators know the time o' the day
From beams reflecting of the solar ray;
Its basis with ascending steps is grac'd,
Around whose area cleanly matrons plac'd,
Vend their most wholesome food, by nature good,
To cheer the spirits and enrich the blood.

One finds it difficult to imagine the rough beef-and-beer Englishman of that period having his "spirits cheered" by "milk, porridge, and broth," but the bard, perhaps, was related to Taylor the "Water-poet."

On May 12, 1671, William, Earl of Bedford, received a grant of the square from Charles II by Letters Patent. In 1679, when it was rated to the poor for the first time, there appear to have been twenty-three salesmen, rated respectively at 2s. and 1s. in the £ (Cunningham).

Probably the earliest allusion to the market is that found in the churchwardens' accounts—date, March 1656—"paid to the painter for painting the benches and seates in the Markett Place, £1 10 0."

In 1666 a payment was also made "for trees planted in the Broad Place," meaning the square in front of the Piazzas. In "The Gentleman's Magazine" of August 20, 1853, appears a copy of the lease between the Earl and certain parties to whom he let the market. It is rather a quaint document, and runs as follows:

"This indenture made the six day of July in the thirteenth yeare of the raigne of Oe Soveraigne Lord Charles The Second, by the grace of God etc., between the Rt Honl William, Earle of Bedford, Lord

Russell, Baron Russell of Thornhaugh, Knight of the most noble order of the Garter, of the one part; and Adam Pigott, Citizen and cutler of London and Thomas Day of the parish of St Clements Danes in the county of Middlesex, tallow-chandler, on the other part." The document continues: "The earl did for the considerations therein mentioned, demise, grant and to ffarme, lett unto the said Adam Pigott and James Allen, all that markett in the parish of St Paul, Covent Garden, etc., to be held every day of the weeke except Sunday and the ffeast day of the birth of our Lord, for buying and selling of all and all manner of fruits and fflowers, roots and herbes whatsoever, and also liberty to build and make cellars and shops all along on the outside of the garden wall of Bedford House garden, so as in such buildings noe chimneys or tunnells be made or putte and soe as such shops be made uniforme in roofs and ffronts one with another and be one ffoote lower than the now garden wall and not above eight foot in Breadth from the wall all alonge the said wall except against the jetty or round of the said wall, against which the said shoppes were to be bt three foote of the most, according to a modell or ground plott of the said buildings to the said recited indenture affixed, together with all other liberties and all tolls, customs, stallage, pittage, and all other p'fitts, comodities, advantages and emoluments whatsoever to the said markett in any wise belonginge or appertaining, ariseing or renewing. The said markett to be kept within the Rayles there and the markett people to sit in order between the said Rayles and the said garden wall from one end to the other end thereof," etc. The same was to date for twenty-one years at the yearly rental "of fourscore pounds of the lawful monies of England."

At this period the Stocks Market was the most important market of the metropolis. It was situated on the site of the present Mansion House, and was established in 1282 by Henry Walis, Lord Mayor. Stow says that the market was named after a pair of stocks which stood here for the punishment of offenders.

Strype writes: "Up farther north is the Stocks Market. As to the present state of which it is converted to a quite contrary use: for instead of Flesh and Fish sold there before the Fire, are now sold Fruits, Roots and Herbs; for which it is very considerable and much resorted unto, being of note for having the choicest of their kind of all sorts, surpassing all other markets in London."

Stocks Market was removed in 1737 to the site of the present Farringdon Street, where it became known as the Fleet Market, doubtless owing to its close proximity to the River Fleet. It still exists under the name of Farringdon Market, but has been quite eclipsed in importance by Covent Garden.

III

*A residential neighbourhood—Emigration of nobility
and gentry from the city—The Piazzas and the critics—
First instance of brick construction—Artistic centre—Sir
Peter Lely, Sir Godfrey Kneller, Sir James Thornhill,
Richard Wilson, Hogarth, Sir Joshua Reynolds, and other
celebrated residents of the Garden—Punch's Theatre—
Sport in the Piazzas—National Sporting Club*

In 1580 Elizabeth, startled at the great increase of the metropolis, issued a proclamation forbidding the erection of any houses but those of the highest class within three miles of the City; and in 1617 James I commanded all noblemen, knights, and gentlemen who had mansions in the country to depart thither, within twenty days of his proclamation, with their wives and families, and to spend the summer vacation there.

Charles I, about the time when the Earl of Bedford commenced the improvement of Covent Garden, the neighbourhood having then first become a residential one, forbade the entertainment of additional inmates in houses already existing. This practice, according to Mr Knight, "would multiply the inhabitants to such an extent that they could neither be governed nor fed."

(Poor Mr Knight! If he could only "revisit the glimpses of the moon" and see our seething metropolis to-day!)

The Earl, however, appears to have disregarded the mandate, and continued his building operations. How he appeased the King is not known. Probably he was fined, and submitted with good grace, as he foresaw his operations would turn into a profitable speculation.

In 1657 an Act was passed by the Protector, Cromwell, "that in regard of the Great Charges that Francis, late Earl of Bedford, hath been at in building a Church in Covent Garden, in the County of Middlesex, and in the endowment of the same Church and other Publick Charges in and about the Parish of Covent Garden aforesaid, there be abated unto William, Earl of Bedford, John Russell and Edward Russell Esquires, Sons of the said Francis, late Earl of Bedford, out of the Fines which shall be payable unto them by force of this Act, in Respect of the Building in the said Parish of Covent Garden, the sum of £7000, the same abatement to be made unto them by the said Commissioners proportionately accordingly as they shall be severally chargeable by this Act" (Strype).

The newly constructed buildings naturally attracted the best people, who even before the Great Fire (1666) were leaving the City to reside in the newer parts of the West End.

Inigo Jones had been busy in the neighbourhood, and on all sides fine mansions had sprung up, and such streets as Drury Lane, Great and Little Queen Street, and Lincoln's Inn Fields became tenanted by noblemen and gentry. These thoroughfares, together with Bow Street, Russell Street, King Street, and Henrietta Street, were in the hey-day of their fashion, just as smart and expensive localities as are Grosvenor Square and Park Lane to-day.

The Piazzas are said to have been copied from that at Livorno in Italy. Being a complete innovation, they became, on the principle of "omne ignotum pro mirifico," one of the show places of the town. The name itself, too, seems to have caught on and become attractive, much in the same way as the old woman expressed her admiration of "that godly word Mesopotamia." Mr Hare, in his "Walks in London," says that the name Piazza was frequently given to foundlings, many of whom were left at the door of the Bishop of Durham, who resided there. It may be doubted whether his Episcopal Holiness was much gratified by these left-handed compliments thus "laid at his door," having probably not so much claim as Charles II to be regarded as "the Father of his people." At any rate, the registers of the time abounded in such names as Peter, Mary, or Paul Piazza.

It was the original intention of the architect that the whole square should be encompassed by this kind of arcade, but the scheme was never carried out in its entirety. In 1783 a book was published entitled "A Critical Review of the Public Buildings and Statues of London and

Westminster," by Ralph, who writes: "Covent Garden would have been, beyond dispute, one of the finest squares in the universe, if finished on the plans that Inigo Jones first designed for it; but even this was neglected too; and if he deserves the praise of the design, we very justly incur the censure for wanting spirit to put it into execution. The Piazza is grand and noble, and the superstructure it supports light and elegant."

The northern portion was called the Great Piazza, and that on the east the Little Piazza. The south-east part of the latter was destroyed by fire in March 1769.

Note that bricks were first commonly used for building purposes in Inigo Jones's time. Previously they had only been used for the construction of chimneys, and occasionally in palaces and monasteries. The Piazzas were one of the first instances of brick construction ("Archæologia," i.). Lilly's "Scriptura" states that the Earl of Arundel was the first who brought over from Italy the new way of building with bricks, "which tended to the safety of the City and the preservation of the wood of the Nation."

The portion west of James Street was pulled down in 1880 and rebuilt by Messrs. Cubbitt.

Most of the contemporary writers, such as Congreve, Wycherley, Otway, Killigrew, Fielding, and Shadwell made use of the Piazzas as a scene of action in their novels and plays; *e.g.* Otway in "The Soldier's Fortune," Wycherley in "The Country Wife."

The present-day observer may find it difficult to imagine to himself Covent Garden as an artistic centre, and yet at the beginning of the eighteenth century it was, par excellence, the haunt of the fashionable portrait-painter. The artistic fraternity, after inhabiting the neighbourhood for a great many years, gradually migrated westward to St Martin's Lane and Leicester Square, whither Sir Joshua Reynolds and Hogarth afterwards removed their studios.

Both Sir Peter Lely and Sir Godfrey Kneller occupied studios in Covent Garden, and were visited by most of the beauties of the court of Charles II. The former lived in the angle of the Piazza now occupied by the Tavistock Hotel. He was born at Soest, in Westphalia, in 1618. His father, an army captain named Van der Faes, was born at a perfumer's shop, at the sign of the Lily, hence was known as Captain du Lys, or Lely. He settled in London in 1641. His best-known works are now at Hampton Court Palace. Included in the collection are the portraits of Lady Bellasis, Frances Stuart, Anne Hyde Duchess of York, the Duchesses of Portsmouth and Cleveland, and the Comtesse de Grammont, which are justly reckoned amongst the art treasures of the nation. Mr Ernest Law writes: "It must be confessed that he has succeeded in giving that voluptuous expression of tender languishment which is so much in harmony with the characters of those beautiful and charming creatures … Their nightgowns fastened with a single pin, and the sleepy eye which spoke the melting soul, would have sufficiently told us their history if the memoir-writers had failed to supply it."

According to Pope, Kneller was one of the vainest of men. Pope once flattered him by saying, "Sir Godfrey, I believe, if the Almighty had had your assistance, the world would have been made more perfect."

"'Fore God, sir," answered the artist, laying his hand upon the poet's shoulder, "I believe so."

Kneller also once remarked to the Bishop of Rochester that the following were his articles of religion: "That God loved all ingenious persons; that painting was the most ingenious of all arts; and that he was the most ingenious of all painters."

Through which beautiful and ingenuous syllogism the love of the Supreme Being is seen to rise in a crescendo scale until it forms a blinding halo on the crown of the artist!

Pope, in his "Satires and Epistles," v. 382, writes:

And great Nassau to Kneller's hand decreed
To fix him graceful on the bounding steed.

This great picture of William III on horseback is now in the Presence Chamber at Windsor.

Several of Kneller's works are at Hampton Court, the more celebrated of which are placed in the King's Presence Chamber, and are known as the Hampton Court Beauties, to distinguish them from Lely's. The latter, having once been at Windsor, are known as the Windsor Beauties.

Kneller's house was on the site of the west end of the Floral Hall, and was described in an advertisement in 1714 as containing a front room 42 ft by 19 ft and 12 ft high, with a garden attached to the mansion 150 ft by 40 ft. The garden adjoined that of the house in which lived Dr Radcliffe in Bow Street. The two were intimate friends, and

Kneller, who was devoted to flowers, had a communicating door made between the two houses. That old gossip Horace Walpole is responsible for the tale that Kneller, annoyed by the plucking of the flowers in his garden by the doctor's servants, sent word that he must close up the door. Radcliffe replied that "he might do anything with it but paint it"; to which the artist answered that "he could take anything from him but physic." Sir James Thornhill afterwards occupied this house, where he opened a drawing-class. He was the first who conceived the admirable idea of a Royal Academy, and proposed that a suitable edifice be erected for the purpose near the King's Mews, now Trafalgar Square. Nothing appears to have come of the scheme just then, and the question seems to have fallen into abeyance.

We are indebted to Sir James for many beautiful frescoes and decorations, the best known of which are the Inner Dome of St Paul's Cathedral, and that in the Great Hall of the Royal Naval College at Greenwich. Several times recently some finely executed ceilings have been discovered in old houses in process of demolition in the neighbourhood of Soho, which have been attributed to him. When he removed to a house in St Martin's Lane, on the site of the present Duke of York's Theatre, he painted in it a magnificent allegorical staircase (Macmichael's "History of Charing Cross").

The other genius whose studio was in the Piazza was Richard Wilson, the friend of Garrick and Arne. Wilson was the unfortunate member of a celebrated trio of painters, *i.e.* Hogarth, Gainsborough, and himself.

Poor Wilson apparently, like many of his confrères, found great trouble in disposing of his paintings. This state of affairs was due to the competition which he had to encounter at the hands of other artists, amongst whom at this time was Barret, who arrived in London in 1761, was received with open arms by the fashionable world (*vide* "Arnold's Magazine," 1832), and was fortunate enough to obtain prices for his works three or four times greater than any ever demanded by Wilson. On one occasion Lord Dalkeith paid Barret 1,500 guineas for three pictures. When Wilson, an exceedingly proud man, advanced his own prices, the sole result was that he did less business than ever. He had quarrelled with Reynolds, and in addition had the misfortune to offend both Royalty and the Court.

A friend wished to bring Wilson's works under the notice of the King, and commissioned him to paint a picture to be submitted to

His Majesty. The subject was a view of Sion House, and the picture was submitted to Lord Bute as the most suitable intermediary for the purpose. Bute, being partial to the Flemish School, pronounced Wilson's work to be a daub, and offered fifty guineas for it instead of the price demanded, sixty. Wilson in a rage exclaimed, "If the King cannot afford to pay so large a sum, I will take it by instalments of £10 at a time." Wilson, growing despondent, eventually drowned his sorrows in drink, and retired, poor, neglected, and sick at heart, to a village in Denbighshire, where he ended his days.

It is as though, reversing the well-known saying of Talleyrand, some one had said to him, "Mais il faut vivre," and he had replied, "Je n'en vois pas la necessité." Not uncommonly is it found that genius and business capacity are not at home together under the same hat.

Hogarth, who was a son-in-law of Sir James Thornhill, and whom Calverley calls "a photographer that flattereth not," also frequented the Piazza studios. It was at Cock's auction-rooms (afterwards occupied by Robins, the prince of word painters) that he exhibited, free to the public, his series of engravings entitled "Marriage à la Mode."

Robins's rooms were afterwards taken over by Mr Harrison, the proprietor of the "Tavistock Breakfast-rooms," in 1787. This establishment was the ancestor of the present Tavistock Hotel, which for many years has enjoyed a great amount of popularity amongst gentlemen of the old-fashioned school, and who prefer the quiet and unpretentious hotel life of their fathers to the marble and tinselled palatial halls which have recently sprung up over London. In 1867 the old red-brick frontage facing the market was stuccoed. The history of the Tavistock Hotel has been written by Mr C.E. Pascoe in 1887, in celebration of its hundredth anniversary.

Zoffany, theatrical portrait painter, also resided in this locality, where he painted Foote in the character of Major Sturgeon.

One of the first residents of the Piazza was Sir Edmund Verney, who took the last two houses on the eastern side (on the site where afterwards stood the Bedford Coffee-house) from the Earl of Bedford at an annual rental of £160. There were coach-houses and stables in the back premises, and it appears from the enumeration of fixtures that, although the ordinary rooms had merely "casements," the principal apartments were distinguished by "shuttynge wyndowes," and that the door of almost every room had its "stock lock."

A reservation was made of the Earl's right to the "walk underneath the same messuage, commonly called the Portico Walk, as the same is now made and perfected by the said Earl," but with power for Sir E. Verney to expel youths playing in the said walk to his offence or disturbance. Parts of the house were "waynscotted," a distinction deemed so important that the use of the same was specifically granted in the lease; and all the separate pieces of "waynscott" were enumerated in the schedule of fixtures. There being as yet no sewer in this new district, Verney fortified himself with a clause that, if he should be so annoyed by that circumstance as not to be able to continue there "with any conveyancy," he might resign his occupation on giving the Earl six months' notice ("Verney Papers," Camden Society MSS., dated November 1, 1634).

Other residents in the Piazza were the Marquis of Winchester in 1645; the Hon. Lady Pye and Sir Charles Cotterell in 1690; the Countess of Peterborough, Sir John Wittwing, Lord Wilmot, Sir W. Udal, and the Earl of Sussex in 1647; Sir H. Vane in 1646; Sir J. Lucas, the Hon. Lord Savage, and Sir Lyon Tallmarch in 1653. Lady Mary Wortley Montagu also resided in the neighbourhood, and was addressed here by Pope.

Mrs Robinson, the actress, familiarly known as "Perdita," and mistress of the Prince of Wales, afterwards George IV (truly "lost" if she put her confidence in such a Prince), lived for some time in the Little Piazza, in a house situated between the Bedford and the Hummums.

In the Little Piazza was Punch's Theatre, where, according to "The Spectator," Martin Powell's performances thinned the congregations of St Paul's Church. Here was acted a mock opera called "Venus and Adonis, or, The Triumph of Love," also "King Bladud," "Friar Bacon and Friar Bungay," "Robin Hood and Little John," and the well-worn pantomime "Mother Goose." The prices of admission to these performances were, boxes 2s. 6d., pit 1s. 6d., and nobody was admitted in masks or riding-cloaks with hoods.

When the fashionable tenants began to desert the neighbourhood, the fine houses were taken over by ladies of doubtful reputation, who turned them into gambling-houses and vicious resorts. The most notorious of these women were Mother Thornton, and Mother Douglas, alias "Coals" (let us hope, in this case too, "not so black as she was painted"). These two matrons occupied premises on the side of the west end of the present Floral Hall.

At the close the seventeenth century the open Market Square was used after business hours as a recreation ground by the apprentices and the children of the neighbourhood. We read in Gay's "Trivia":

> Where Covent Garden's famous temple stands,
> That boasts the work of Jones' immortal hands,
> Here oft my course I bend, when lo! from far
> I spy the furies of the football war;
> The prentice quits his shop to join the crew,
> Increasing crowds the flying game pursue, etc.

Mention also is made of cricket being played here.

The Piazzas do not appear to have been built any too solidly. An old History of London says that a good many repairs have taken place owing to some errors in the foundations, "which have occasioned derangements in the perpendicular of the fronts; hence they are under continual repair."

At the west end of the Piazza, adjoining King Street, is a building which has existed since 1636. This building, probably one of the most interesting in the whole of the vicinity, is the National Sporting Club. Like other houses in Covent Garden, it was originally the town residence, in turn, of many persons of note. The first tenant was William Alexander, Earl of Stirling; and he was followed consecutively by Thomas Killigrew, Denzil Holles, and Sir Henry Vane.

The house was afterwards occupied by Sir Kenelm Digby, son of that unfortunate Sir Everard Digby who had been concerned in the abhorred Gunpowder Plot, and had suffered the penalty of his crime by being hanged, drawn, and quartered in St Paul's Churchyard. Sir Kenelm, besides having been a foreign envoy ("vir bonus, peregrè missus ad mentiendum reipublicæ causâ"), was an amateur chemist, and was celebrated for inventing a cure for sword wounds. He must have been somewhat of a Christian Scientist, for his prescription was to anoint the sword, not the wound. The ingenuous novelty of this treatment has drawn from Mr Bettinson, of the National Sporting Club, the humorous prescription of "boxing-gloves bathed in warm water, and plastered with gold-beater's skin" as a cure for bruises (History of the Club, by Fitzgerald).

After the death of Digby the premises became the residence of Admiral Russell, Earl of Orford, who in 1692 defeated the French under Admiral de Tourville at La Hogue. He altered and renovated the exterior of the building in such a manner that many declared the nautical character of the tenant was apparent in his alterations, comparing the new exterior to the hull of a ship. The bluff sailor himself would probably have been content to admit that he was making it "ship-shape."

Soon afterwards the house became the scene of the first Cabinet Council ever held in this country. "One of the methods employed by the Whig Junto for the purpose of instituting and maintaining through all the ranks of the Whig party a discipline never before known was the frequent holding of meetings of the members of the House of Commons. Some of these meetings were numerous, others select. The large ones were held at the Rose, the smaller at Russell's in Covent Garden" (Macaulay).

The next tenant was Thomas, Lord Archer (d. 1768); and after him came James West, the great collector of books, prints, drawings, etc. When these were sold the auctioneer took six weeks to dispose of them. West was President of the Royal Society, and died in 1772. The premises were opened in 1774 by David Low as a family hotel, which is said to have been the first of its kind in London. The next landlord caused great amusement by advertising the hotel "with stabling for one hundred noblemen and horses." If all we read about the noblemen of those times and their manners and customs at table be correct, the horses would certainly have more cause to complain of their associates than the noblemen.

In the garden of the house was a small cottage inhabited by the Kemble family. It was here that the gifted Fanny Kemble was born. The present hall of the club stands on the site. The hotel afterwards became the famous Evans's Supper Rooms, where Bohemian London nightly gathered, and where the old chairman presided with the hammer. There many a good old-fashioned glee, such as "The Chough and Crow," and many a cheery chorus, was sung; there many, a succulent kidney and devilled bone, not unaccompanied by the flouriest of baked potatoes, were consumed in the good old days of long ago.

Where did those potatoes grow? No earthly soil produced them—so spotlessly white, so crumbly, so creamy. If Alice had cultivated a garden in Wonderland, they might have come from it. But Evans has gone, and has carried the secret of those potatoes away into the Ewigkeit.

Can any one who has read Thackeray's "The Newcomes" fail to picture to himself the scene (evidently taken from Evans's) where the

lean old wiry Colonel takes his boy for an evening's innocent amusement, spoilt at the end by a ribald song from Captain Costigan; and
the veteran's fierce exit with bristling moustache and uplifted cane,
"which," as the narrator said, "seemed to fall on the shoulders of every
one of us"?

IV

*St Paul's Church—Cost and date of construction—Inigo
Jones—Consecration ceremony—Dispute between
the Earl of Bedford and the Vicar of the parish of St
Martin's-in-the-fields—Criticisms on the church—First
destructive fire—Celebrated persons buried there—The
churchyard—The Actors' Church—Tom King's coffee-
house—The hustings: exciting scenes—The "Finish"—
Statue of Charles I at Charing Cross*

The parish church of St Paul is perhaps the most interesting spot in
the vicinity of Covent Garden. Built in 1633, it has suffered many
vicissitudes, being on one occasion almost totally destroyed by fire.
Fortunately it was completely restored, and it still dominates the busy
market of to-day, as it has done since its erection.

It was built by Inigo Jones, to the order of Francis, Earl of Bedford.
Pennant ascribes it to the second Earl—a statement which is contra-
dicted by Horace Walpole, who writes: "I conclude Earl Francis, who
died in 1641, was the builder, as the church was not erected till after
the Civil War began." Mr Peter Cunningham agrees with Walpole,
who was undoubtedly correct in his statement.

An old story with reference to church, believed to have originated
with Walpole, runs to the effect that the Earl did not wish to incur too
great an expense in its construction, and so told the architect that he
"did not wish for a building much bigger than a barn"; to which Jones
is reported to have answered, "Then, you shall have the handsomest
barn in England."

The cost of the edifice was £4,500. To obtain the relative purchasing power of coin in those days, compared with that in our own, it is quite reasonable to multiply the sums by ten. The cost therefore was considerable. The building was not consecrated till 1638. The delay was caused by a dispute between the Earl and Mr Bray, vicar of St Martin's-in-the-Fields, as to the right of presentation.

"Londinium Redivivum" gives a full account of the proceedings, which were held before the King in Council at Whitehall on April 6, 1638, when a petition addressed to His Majesty, and signed by one hundred inhabitants of Covent Garden, was read. The petition stated that the parish church of St Martin's had become small for the inhabitants of the newer neighbourhood of Covent Garden, which edifice was fit to be parochial, "whither the new inhabitants, without trouble of the other, might resort to their service of God."

The Earl gave it as his opinion that, as he had presented the ground and erected the church at his own cost, and promised £100 a year to the minister as an extra remuneration, he ought to be the Patron, and to nominate "a clerk" to the living. The Vicar, holding that Covent Garden and all its recently erected buildings were in the parish of St Martin's, and that the new church, when consecrated, could not be made parochial without an express Act of Parliament, insisted on the right of nominating a curate himself, undertaking to allow him 100 marks a year. The decision was given in the Earl's favour, the King ordering a special Act to be passed making the church parochial, and giving to the Earl and his heirs full and legal right to the presentation and patron age of the said church.

In 1660 the first Act of Parliament passed provided that the church and parish of St Paul's, Covent Garden, should hence forth be separated from that of St Martin's-in-the-Fields.

The following act was signed by the Earl: "In the name of God, Amen. Know all me present and to come that I, Francis Bedford, for me and my heirs, have offered up in memory of the Blessed Apostle, St Paul, all this plat or piece of ground, containing in length from the East to the West 251 feet, in breadth from the North part towards the South 145 feet and 3 inches; together with three ingrediences or passages unto the same plat; one part whereof leading out of the same plat, etc., being situated in the precinct called Convent Garden in the parish of St Martin's-in-the-Fields, upon one part whereof one structure in the form of a church or chapel is erected and built at my charges, and the other is enclosed, now with a brick wall, that the dead within the precinct of Convent Garden, and with one house, commonly called Bedford House, may be therein buried, together with the said structure in form of a church or chapel, and the said plat or piece of ground may be consecrated and applied for sacred prayers, the preaching of the Holy Word, for the Sacraments and sacramental use of the inhabitants in the precincts of Convent Garden and within my house called Bedford House for ever. In testimony whereof I have put my seal of arms to these presents. Dated the 26th day of the month of September, *anno domini* 1638, and in the reign of our Lord Charles, by the Grace of God," etc.

The consecration ceremony was at length performed by Juxon, Bishop of London, the same who attended Charles I on the scaffold. The building is in the Tuscan style of architecture, probably made familiar to Jones when pursuing his artistic studies in Italy in his early days.

Mr W.J. Loftie writes that the portico is a mere adjunct to the square and no integral part of the church. The same authority states that the edifice was almost entirely rebuilt in 1688, a few years after its erection. The reason is not known.

The style of the finished building has evoked criticisms of several kinds.

"The barn roof over the portico of the church strikes my eyes with as little dignity or beauty as it could do if it covered nothing but a barn. In justice to Inigo, one must own that the defect is not in the architect, but in the order; whoever saw a beautiful Tuscan building? Would the Romans have chosen that order for a temple?" (Horace Walpole).

John Noorthouck, in his History of London, writes: "This church has the rare good fortune to be placed where it is seen to advantage; it stands on the west side of a fine square, the area of which is the greatest market for greens, fruits, and flowers in the metropolis."

The architect himself must have had a good opinion of his work, as he "desired by his will, that on his monument in the Church of St Benet's, Paul's Wharf, should be placed views in relief of the portico of St Paul's Cathedral and the church in Covent Garden" (Loftie's "Wren and Inigo Jones").

In 1725 Lord Burlington, himself an amateur architect of no mean skill, restored the portico at a cost of between three and four hundred pounds; and in 1788 the walls were encased in Portland stone, and the rustic gates at the west end were rebuilt in stone.

In 1795 the beautiful ceiling, the work of E. Pierce, a pupil of the great master Van Dyck, a portrait of Charles I by Lely, and the windows and roof were destroyed by fire. Happily the walls and portico escaped total destruction, and the whole edifice was subsequently restored by Hardwicke Senior. On its reconstruction, the consecration ceremony was performed by the Bishop of London, attended by the Archdeacon of St Paul's.

The church was originally insured for £10,000 at the Westminster Fire Office, but the policy had expired just a year, and since it had not been renewed, the loss fell on the parish, and drove up rents at least twenty-five per cent. (Allen's "London").

The church boasted the first long-pendulum clock in Europe, which was designed and made by Richard Harris, of London, in 1641 (Timbs). In 1888 the west-end turret was removed, and a high iron railing now replaces, on the east side, the old wall and arches.

St Paul's Church, Covent Garden, shelters the remains of many celebrated personages; in fact it is said, that, with the exception of Westminster Abbey and St Paul's Cathedral, no other church in London can boast of so many famous people sleeping peacefully within its precincts. The list commences with the name of Robert Carr, Earl of Somerset, who was buried here probably on account of his relationship with the Russell family, his daughter having married William, afterwards Duke of Bedford. To Butler, the author of "Hudibras", whose friends could not afford to bury him in Westminster Abbey, a marble monument was placed in 1786 on the inside south wall of the church, with this inscription:

"This little monument was erected in the year 1786; by some of the parishioners of Covent Garden, in memory of the celebrated Samuel Butler, who was buried in this church, A.D. 1680.

A few plain men, to pomp and state unknown,
O'er a poor bard have raised this humble stone;
Whose wants alone his genius could surpass—
Victim of zeal! The matchless Hudibras!
What though fair freedom suffer'd in his page,
Reader, forgive the author for the age!

How few, alas! disdain to cringe and cant
When 'tis the mode to play the sycophant.
But oh! let all be taught from Butler's fate,
Who hope to make their fortunes by the great,
That wit and pride are always dangerous things,
And little faith is due, to courts and kings.

In 1721 a monument was erected to Butler in Westminster Abbey by Alderman Barber. Upon its epitaph Samuel Wesley wrote the following stinging lines:

While Butler, needy wretch, was still alive,
No generous patron would a dinner give.
See him, when starved to death, and turned to dust,
Presented with a monumental bust.
The poet's fate is here in emblem shown;
He asked for bread, and he received a stone.

Sir Peter Lely the painter, Wycherley the dramatist, Eastcourt the actor, Dr. Arne the musician, Tom King (the original Sir Peter Teazle, in "The School for Scandal"), Sir Robert Strange the engraver (who resided in Henrietta Street, to whose memory a tablet on the south wall is inscribed), Mrs Davenport, Edward Kynaston the actor of female parts, Grinling Gibbons the sculptor, John Godfrey Kneller, brother of Sir Godfrey Kneller, Mrs Centlivre the witty dramatist, Thomas Girton the father of water-colour painting, John Walcott ("Peter Pindar," whose grave is adjacent to that of Butler), and Macklin the comedian (who died in 1797 at the advanced age of 107), make up a goodly company of illustrious dead interred here.

Macklin's tablet reads as follows:

SACRED TO THE MEMORY OF
CHARLES MACKLIN
Comedian.
THIS TABLET IS ERECTED
(With the aid of public patronage)
By his affectionate widow Eliz. Macklin.
Obiit 11th July, 1797, ætatis 107.

> Macklin, the Father of the modern stage,
> Renowned alike for talent and for age,
> Whose years a century and longer ran,
> Who lived and died as may become a man;
> This lasting tribute to thy work receive,
> 'Tis all a grateful public now can give,
> Their loudest plaudits now no more can move,
> Yet hear thy widow's still small voice of love.

Another centenarian buried here is Marmaduke Conway, a faithful servant of James I, and a favourite of Charles I on account of his skill in hawking. He died in 1717, aged 108 years and a few months.

There is also a very old memorial stone affixed to the north wall, dated 1648. It reads in old characters:

"Here under lieth ye body of Mary Ffenn, late wife of John Ffenn, who departed this life ye 14th of September, 1648.

> Reader look heare, a Wonder
> Amongst men, Thou tread'st upon
> An odoriferous Ffenn.
> A pious, virtuous chaste
> Religious wife, Expecting
> Resurrection, Left this Life.

Here was christened Lady Mary Wortley Montagu in 1690; here, too, the great artist Turner was baptized May 14, 1775. Both his parents are buried under the nave. He himself was buried in St Paul's Cathedral.

There is a story told of a lady who was looking at Turner's picture of Covent Garden, who remarked, "Well, Mr Turner, I see Covent Garden as often as you do, but truly I cannot see it as you do." To which the great artist replied, "Don't you wish you could, madam?"

Closterman, the artist and competitor of Kneller, is also interred in this church. He was commissioned to paint the family of the great Duke of Marlborough. The Duchess, however, wrangled with him so much over the work that the Duke told him that: "It has given me more trouble to reconcile my wife and you than to fight a battle" (Leigh Hunt's "The Town").

In 1791 Claude Duval, the notorious highwayman, was executed

at Tyburn, and the body, after lying in state in a tavern in St Giles',
was conveyed here, and buried with much pomp in the middle nave.
"The funeral," says Mr Timbs, "was attended by flambeaux and a large
crowd of mourners, amongst whom figured many of the "fair sex."
His epitaph runs:

> Here lies Duval, Reader, if male thou art
> Look to thy purse, if female, to thy heart.

A memorial stone is affixed to the north wall in memory of John
Bellamy, father of the Whig Club of England. In the churchyard are
buried a Richard Gibson and his wife Anne, two dwarfs, each 3 ft. 10
in. high. Gibson was page to Charles I, in whose presence, together
with that of his Queen, the diminutive couple were married. He died
at the age of seventy-five, while his wife lived till 1709, at which date
she was eighty-nine years old. This small couple had nine children,
none of them showing any tendency to reproduce the abnormally
short stature of their parents.

The churchyard has now been paved over and set out as a kind of
garden, which provides a quiet and peaceful oasis of retreat from the
noise and hubbub of the adjacent market. This spot, however, was
described in 1850 as "a plague-spot of human flesh and human remains;
the narrow place of sepulchre of two centuries of the inhabitants of
this parish." A stone on the south side records the fact that the burial-
ground was closed in 1853; two years later permission was given for
the laying flat of the head- and foot-stones of the graves and otherwise
improving the ground.

St Paul's has often been designated "the Actors' Church," and in this
church was solemnised the marriage of Lady Susan Fox-Strangways
(daughter of the Earl of Ilchester, and only just of age) with the handsome and accomplished actor O'Brien, of Drury Lane Theatre, which,
when it became known, was a piece of news that startled fashionable London in 1764. Horace Walpole was sadly upset on hearing
about it, and wrote to the Earl of Hertford that the bride's father,
Lord Ilchester, "was almost distracted; indeed, it is the completion of
disgrace—even a footman were preferable; the publicity of the hero's
profession perpetuates the mortification. I could not have believed
Lady Susan would have stooped so low."

Perhaps the acute distress of these high-born dilettanti may have had the edge taken off it by the fact that O'Brien, after his nuptials, settled down in the country, and no longer thrust "the publicity of his profession betwixt the wind and their nobility." The letter, however, points out very forcibly the status of the actor at that period, and indicates a strong contrast with the honour and titles conferred upon that profession to-day.

It was in this church also that John Rich, proprietor and lessee of Covent Garden Theatre, was married to his third wife, Mrs Priscilla Stevens, a lady who was formerly his housekeeper.

In the churchyard is also buried Betty Careless, a lady of very doubtful (or should not the adjective be "undoubted"?) reputation, who flourished between 1720 and 1740. She was thought of sufficient importance, writes Besant, to receive a brief obituary notice in "The Gentleman's Magazine" of April 1752: "Was buried from the Poor-house of St Paul's, Covent Garden, the famed Betty Careless, who had helped the gay gentlemen of this country to squander £50,000."

Alas, poor Betty! From £50,000 to the poor-house! Sooner or later "the way of the transgressor" is generally made "hard" for him.

The churchyard is also the reputed place of burial of the original (whoever he may have been) of Thackeray's Captain Costigan. It is said that from a window of Offley's in Henrietta Street, which overlooked the churchyard, some of his former boon companions were wont to pour tumblers of punch over his grave. Possibly in his then condition he would have preferred a drop of cold water to the burning fiery liquid of his unregenerate days!

The hustings for the Westminster elections, were placed in front of the church till a comparatively recent date, and many an exciting scene and encounter were witnessed between members of the rival factions.

Great excitement prevailed here in 1784, when the Tories tried their utmost to exclude the Whig leader, Charles James Fox, from Westminster. Thanks to the untiring energy of Georgina, Duchess of Devonshire, and her sister Lady Duncannon, who went round in their carriages canvassing the voters, they gained so many votes for Fox by their charm and beauty that he soon obtained a large majority over his opponent, Sir Cecil Wrey. "The Duchess of Devonshire is indefatigable in her canvass for Fox; she was in the most blackguard houses in Long Acre by eight o'clock this morning" (Letter from Dr Cornwallis, April 9, 1784).

At the close of the poll Fox had a clear majority of 200 votes, in spite of the counter-efforts of the Countess of Salisbury.

It was on this occasion that a witty costermonger respectfully approached the Duchess, who was one of the leading beauties of the day, and asked permission to light his pipe at her ladyship's eye.

After the result of the poll had been announced, Fox was carried through the streets, shoulder-high, to the doors of Carlton House. Contemporary writers have stated that so great was the interest taken in the contest, and so keen was the party feeling, that for three weeks the neighbourhood of the market was the scene of riot and bloodshed.

In front of the church was "Tom King's Coffee-house," a place of considerable repute in those days. It was here that all the town rakes used to congregate in the small hours of the morning. The place was nightly frequented by noblemen and beaux dressed in their finest clothes and who freely mixed with the heterogeneous company commonly met with in a market-place. Tom King was the son of well-to-do parents and was born at West Ashton in Yorkshire. In 1713 he ran away from Eton, where he was being educated, in apprehension that his fellowship would be denied him (Horwood's "Alumni Etonenses").

On Tom's death, the place was carried on by his widow, Moll King, under whose management it gained such an unsavoury reputation that a contemporary poet dedicated the following lines to it:

Where a wide area opens to the sight
A spacious Plain quadrangularly right,
Whose large frontiers with the Pallisado's bound
From Trivia's filth enshrines the hallow'd ground
In which Pomono keeps her fruitful court
And youthful Flora with her Nymphs resort.

At length the scandal became so great that steps were taken to put an end to the trouble. In a newspaper cutting of May 24, 1739, we read: "Yesterday, Moll King, mistress of Tom King's Coffee-house, Covent Garden, was brought to the King's Bench to receive judgment, when the Court committed her to the King's Bench prison, Southwark, till they took time to consider of a punishment adequate to the offence." On June 9th of the same year, she was fined £200 and imprisoned for three months and to find security for her good behaviour for three years and to remain in prison until the fine be paid. This was the maximum sentence for keeping a disorderly house. Another tavern of note was the "Finish," originally the "Queen's, Head," kept by Mrs Butler, which was on the south side of the market. It eventually became the resort of footpads and highwaymen, besides being patronised by the young bloods, who found it convenient, to wind up an evening's debauch at a place which was not closed all night. J.P. Kemble, in a merry (perhaps exalted) mood, once visited the place and insisted on speaking a few lines from his new part, Coriolanus. The voluntary effusion was unpalatable to the company, who "rose at him," with the result that he made an exit O.P. more hurried than dignified.

The following lines referring to the "Finish" were written by Tom Moore in Tom Cribb's "Memorial to Congress":

> Some place that's like the 'Finish,' lads!
> Where all your high pedestrian pads,
> That have been up and out all night
> Running their rigs among the rattlers,
> At morning meet and, honour bright,
> Agree to share the blunt and taters.

The "Finish" was the last of the Covent Garden night taverns, and was cleared away in 1829.

It appears that the statue of Charles I which now stands at the top of Whitehall was once concealed in the vaults of St Paul's Church, Covent Garden. When the King was executed, Parliament gave orders for the statue to be destroyed, and handed it over to a brazier named Rivett with instructions to that effect. The latter conceived the brilliant idea of storing it away until better (i.e. more monarchical) times should arrive. In order, however, to give foundation to the idea that he had broken it up, he made small bronzes and vases, which he sold as manufactured out of the material of the original statue. These were eagerly purchased by both Royalist and Roundhead: the latter regarding them as souvenirs of their triumphs, the former as cherished mementoes of their dead monarch. At the Restoration, Rivett was induced to give up the statue ("History of Charing Cross", by Macmichael).

V

Russell Street and the coffee-houses—Their history and importance—The first coffee-house in London—Wills's, Buttons', Tom's, the Bedford, the Rose—John Dryden— Pope—The assault on Dryden—Various descriptions of Wills's—"The Tatler"—Richard Steele and Joseph Addison—"The Guardian" and "The Spectator"

Russell Street was for some considerable period the chief thoroughfare in Covent Garden. Before the improvements in the neighbourhood it gave direct access to the theatre in Drury Lane from the west end of the town. From the time of its construction in 1634 down to the period of the latter Georges its importance may be reckoned as on a par with that of Pall Mall to-day.

The chief attraction of this street was the presence there of the coffee-houses which sprang into public favour about 1660. The advent of these houses supplied a long-felt want. At that period nothing like our present newspaper was in existence; consequently the opening of the coffee-houses provided facilities for all parties to meet and discuss the political and social news of the day. Every man of the better classes had his favourite haunt, whither he adjourned for a few hours' recreation from business. There, over a cup of coffee, he joined in the general conversation, which in some establishments reached quite a high standard of literary debate. It cannot be denied that the coffee-houses played a most important rôle in the morals of the period, substituting, as they did, an innocuous drink in the place of the alcoholic temptations of the general tavern. In our own day the tea-shops have done more for the cause of temperance than any amount of preaching or cerulean decorations. It is a well-established fact that the tea-shop attracts many, who once patronised the public-houses, to the quiet and modest resort where any decent woman can show her face, and where for a reasonable sum light refreshment is provided, and a game of chess or draughts can be enjoyed.

The first coffee-house was established in London in 1652, and was situated in St Michael's Alley, Cornhill.

A certain merchant, who travelled in the East, returned from a journey, bringing with him an Oriental servant, who used to prepare a cup of coffee for his master every morning. Some time afterwards this domestic conceived the idea of opening a shop for the sale of this novelty. He joined his fortunes with the coachman of his late employer, and the two set up for themselves at the address above mentioned.

The custom of coffee-drinking spread with remarkable swiftness. In 1660 a duty of 4d. was levied on every gallon of coffee made or sold. Coffee-houses sprang up in every direction, and three years later it was ordained that they should be licensed at Quarter Sessions.

So popular did these establishments become that the authorities suspected them of providing facilities for the preaching of treason. Charles II even went so far as to command the closing of these places of resort; but the decree was afterwards repealed.

The most important of the Covent Garden houses were Wills's, Buttons', Tom's, the Bedford, and the Rose. The two former were the most celebrated.

Wills's was situated at the west corner of Bow Street and Russell Street. It was formerly a tavern, known as the Red Cow, according to Sir Walter Scott, and afterwards as the Rose. It is to be observed, however, that this latter appellation was common to such places of entertainment.

The landlord, Mr William Urwin, seeing how popular coffee-drinking had become, turned his place into a coffee-house. The name was altered to "Wills's," and the place eventually became the most important centre of serious literary discussion. Dryden was the great man of genius, who was in fact the *genius loci* there. He became the "cynosure of neighbouring" wits; he made the fortune of the house; young and old flocked by day and night to bask in the sunshine of his wit; and great was the pride of any one favoured with a pinch of snuff from his venerated snuff-box.

Pope, when a lad, had conceived such a feeling of respect for Dryden, that he pestered his friends to take him to Wills's that he might gaze upon the great man. His delight was great when his wish had at last been gratified. He afterwards described him as a "plump man with a down look, and not very conversible."

Dryden was born on August 9, 1631, in a Northampton village which rejoiced in the quaint name of Aldwinkle All Saints. Sprung from well-connected parents, he was educated at Westminster School, and afterwards at Cambridge, where he entered Trinity College in 1650. He matriculated a few months later, and at the end of that year was elected to a Westminster scholarship. He was married December 1, 1663, to Lady Elizabeth Howard, eldest daughter of the Earl of Berkshire. His appearance at Wills's may be said to have commenced within a year of his marriage (Saintsbury's "Life of Dryden"). Pepys writes that he was stopped, as he was going to fetch his wife, at the great coffee-house in Covent Garden, "and there found Dryden, the poet I knew at Cambridge, and all the wits of the Town."

The poet's place of honour at Wills's was by the fireside in winter, and during the summer months a chair on the balcony overlooking the street. His plays were produced at the Theatre Royal, Drury Lane, and he resided in Gerrard Street near St Martin's Lane, and also in Rose Street, Long Acre.

It was in the latter street on December 18, 1679, that Dryden was the victim of a cowardly assault at the hands of a band of masked bullies, or Mohocks, as these desperadoes were then called. He was returning home, probably from Wills's, when he was attacked and severely maltreated. A reward of £50 was offered for the discovery of his assailants, and the money was lodged at Temple Bar with the firm now known as Child's Bank. The reward produced no effect, but popular belief ascribed the outrage to Wilmot, Earl of Rochester. It appears that Dryden was on friendly terms with Lord Mulgrave, formerly a great friend of, but subsequently on bad terms with, Rochester. Shortly after the quarrel a satire was circulated which contained violent attacks on the Earl, the Duchesses of Cleveland and Portsmouth, and even on the King himself. Dryden's biographer, Mr Saintsbury, cannot understand why suspicion ever fell upon the poet on this account. "Firstly," says Mr Saintsbury, "Dryden had never at anytime hired himself out as a literary bravo to any private person; and, secondly, it seems inconceivable that he should attack the King, who was his greatest benefactor.

Thirdly, the style of the offending manuscript was totally unlike that of Dryden."

The following extract will give a vivid illustration of the life at the famous coffee-house: "From thence we adjourned to the Wits' coffee-house … accordingly upstairs we went and found much company, but little talk … we shuffled through the moving crowds of philosophical mutes to the other end of the room, where three or four wits of the upper class were rendez-vous'd at a table, and were disturbing the ashes of the old poets by perverting their sense. … At another table were seated a parcel of young raw beaux and wits, who were conceited if they had but the honour to dip a finger and thumb into Mr Dryden's snuff-box" ("The London Spy").

Macaulay, in his "History of England", writes: "Nowhere was the smoking more constant than at Wills's. That celebrated house, situated between Covent Garden and Bow Street, was sacred to polite letters. There the talk was about poetical justice and the unities of time and place. There was a faction for Perrault and the Moderns, a faction for Boileau and the Ancients. One group debated whether 'Paradise Lost' ought not to have been in rhyme. To another an envious poet-aster demonstrated that 'Venice Preserved' ought to have been hooted from the stage. Under no roof was a greater variety of figures to be seen. There were Earls in stars and garters, clergymen in cassocks and bands, pert Templars, sheepish lads from the Universities, translators and index-makers in ragged coats of frieze. The great press was to get near the chair where John Dryden sate. To bow to the Laureate and to hear his opinion of Racine's last tragedy, or of Bossu's treatise on Epic Poetry, was thought a privilege. A pinch from his snuff-box was an honour sufficient to turn the head of a young enthusiast."

Prior, in his "Town and Country Mouse", describes the scene as follows:

'As I remember,' said the sober mouse,
'I've heard much talk of the wits' coffee-house.'
'Thither,' says Brindle, 'thou shalt go and see
Priests sipping coffee, sparks and poets tea;
Here rugged frieze, there Quality well drest,
These baffling the Grand-Seigneur, those the Test;
And here shrewd guesses made, and reasons given
That human laws were never made in Heaven.

But above all, what shall oblige thy sight,
And fill thy eyeballs with a vast delight,
Is the Poetic-Judge of sacred wit,
Who does i' th' darkness of his glory sit. ...

When publishing the prospectus of his new paper, "The Tatler," Steele wrote: "All accounts of gallantry, pleasure, and entertainment shall be under the article of White's Chocolate House; poetry under that of Wills's Coffee-House; learning under the title of Grecian; foreign and domestic news you will have from the St James' Coffee-House."

Dryden died on May 1, 1710, and a splendid funeral was appointed for him, several peers volunteering to defray the entire cost themselves. The body was embalmed, and, after lying for some days at the Royal College of Physicians, was buried on May 13 in Westminster Abbey.

The lower portion of Wills's was used as a shop, and in 1693 it was let to a woollen draper, by name Philip Brent. In 1722 the premises were occupied by a bookseller named James Woodman, who called his shop "The Camden's Head."

Buttons' came into existence on the opposite side of the street. This celebrated house was named after its proprietor, Mr Buttons, who had at one time been a retainer in the family of the Countess of Warwick. She, on her marriage with Addison, set Buttons up as the landlord of the house, which soon afterwards became the headquarters of the Whig *literati*.

At this period a notable change was passing over the general literature of the day. Men of wit, formerly, were engaged principally in writing and publishing lampoons, satires, and panegyrics. This style of literature, however much amusement it might cause, can hardly be reckoned as attaining to a high place in letters. The shirt of Nessus, the taint of the coarseness of Restoration literature, clung to its poisoned skin. Not long before Dryden's demise there rose above the horizon the clear bright star of a very different class of writings. The earliest of these was "The Tatler", which was followed in due order by "The Spectator" and "The Guardian". The latter publication emanated from "Buttons'", which was constituted the receiving office for all contributions intended for its pages.

"The Tatler" appeared in the spring of 1709, and was a long-cherished and deeply considered venture of Steele. Unlike those of its contemporary rivals, its columns were not exclusively occupied with foreign and political intelligence, although its editor had ample opportunities for making use of such information.

Macaulay writes that Steele "had been appointed Gazetteer by Sunderland at the request, it is said, of Addison, and thus had access to foreign news earlier, and more authentic than any in those times within the reach of an ordinary news-writer."

The main object, however, of the paper was to fill a void in the literary publications of the period. The idea was to bring out a chatty periodical. Addison, being consulted, at once fell in with the suggestion, and his contributions, the earlier as well as the later, received the most favourable notice.

The effect of Addison's assistance cannot be described better than in Steele's own words. "I fared," said he, "like a distressed prince who calls in a powerful neighbour to his aid. I was outdone by my auxiliary. When I had called him in, I could not subsist without dependence on him." "The paper," he says elsewhere, "was advanced indeed. It was raised to a greater thing than I intended it" (Macaulay's "Life of Addison").

"The Tatler" was due to appear three times a week—Tuesdays, Thursdays, and Saturdays, these being the days on which the post left town for the country. Its chief novelty lay in the articles for both sexes. For the ladies there was fashionable intelligence on dress, etc., and for the gentlemen, gossip on the literary news at Wills's, criticisms on the latest theatrical production, and, in short, "such light topics as would pleasantly while away the time spent over coffee and tobacco" (Alex. Charles Ewald, F.S.A.).

The paper lasted two years, having changed, as Macaulay observes, from its original purpose to a collection of essays on books, morals, and manners. The last issue appeared on January 11, 1711. "The Spectator" made its first bow to the public two months later, and was, from the very first, a conspicuous success. The papers, or collection of essays, contain such beautiful and lifelike sketches of character, that the work has all the interest of a modern novel. It may be said to have owed much of its popularity to the fact that it was the first example of a powerful illustration of the life and manners of England.

Richardson and Fielding had not yet entered the literary arena, and Smollett was not yet born. It may be conjectured that the literary birth of all three owes much to their intellectual progenitor, Addison.

"The Spectator" came to an end at the conclusion of 1712. "The Guardian" succeeded it, but enjoyed only a brief existence.

In 1714 a new series of "The Spectator" appeared, in which are to be found, so modern critics assert, some of the finest essays in the English language.

The glory of Addison is to have taught a corrupt age that it is possible to be witty and humorous without being coarse and profligate; to turn the laugh to the side of the honest man away from the side of the knave and seducer; in fact, to steal from the devil, as Luther proposed to do, some of his best tunes.

VI

*The celebrated lion's head at Buttons'—The life of
a man of letters in the seventeenth and eighteenth
centuries—Ambrose Phillips and Pope—The Rose: its
correct situation—Pepys' description—Tom's, and its
fashionable clientele—Tom Davies and Boswell—Dr
Samuel Johnson—Charles Lamb—His appreciation
of the neighbourhood—The Hummums—Dr Johnson's
famous ghost story—The Bedford and its history—David
Garrick—The Piazza Coffee-house—Present-day
Russell Street—Hooper's Pharmacy and the credulous
costermonger—The Harp*

"Buttons'", as before stated, was appointed the receiving place for all contributions to "The Guardian", for which purpose a lion's head was set up at the coffee-house, as a sort of pillar-box. It was taken from the antique Egyptian lion, and was designed by Hogarth.

It was inscribed as follows:

Cervantur magnis isti cervicibus ungues
Non nisi delicta pascitur ille fera.

About this inscription it may be observed that, though both the lines are from Martial, they are not consecutive, but come from two separate epigrams, 23 and 61 in Book I. These epigrams are both on the same subject, and treat of the curious practice of training a lion to allow a hare to run in and out of its jaws unharmed.

There is further a misprint in each line quoted. In line 1 *Cervantur*

should be *Servantur*, and in line 2 *delicta* should be *delecta*. The intention of the couplet, doubtless, is that "The Guardian" proposes to be a
guardian of the lowly and innocent, and intends to strike only at the
"necks of the mighty."

This lion's head was afterwards removed to the Shakespeare Tavern
under the Piazza; in 1804 it was sold to Mr Richardson, the proprietor
of Richardson's Hotel, for £17 10*s*., and eventually purchased by the
Duke of Bedford.

In the eighteenth century the pecuniary benefits to be gained by
a literary career were of the most slender description. Fees paid to
authors were so small that the scanty wage scarce sufficed to keep the
wolf from the door. It is small wonder that many literary men degenerated into spongers and habitués of the Debtors' Prison in the Fleet.
If by chance substantial results followed upon some fleeting smile of
Fortune, it is not surprising, that the unlooked-for opportunity was
immediately abused by the usually penniless and starving scribe.

"All order was destroyed; all business was suspended. The most good-
natured host began to repent of his eagerness to serve a man of genius in
distress, when he heard his guest roaring for fresh punch at five o'clock
in the morning" (Crocker's edition of the "Life of Johnson").

Some few were more successful. Both Pope and Young were patronised by influential people. On the other hand, four of the most
distinguished writers of the time—viz. Johnson, Wycherley, Collins,
and Fielding—were all, at one period of their career, arrested for debt.
It is to the everlasting credit of Steele that he was prompted to encour-
age young authors by affording them facilities to submit their work to
a competent and unbiassed authority.

It was at Buttons' that Ambrose Phillips, a wit and a favourite of
Addison, hung up a birch rod with which he threatened to chastise
Pope for having written an uncomplimentary epigram about him. Mr
Cibber wrote to Pope: "When you used to pass your hours at Buttons',
you were even then remarkable for your satirical itch of provocation;
scarce was there a gentleman of any pretentions to wit whom your
unguarded temper had not fallen upon in some biting epigram; among
whom you once caught a pastoral Tartar, whose resentment, that your
punishment might be proportioned to the smart of your poetry, had
stuck up a birchen rod in the room, to be ready whenever you might
come within reach of it; and at this rate you writ and rallied and writ
on till you rhymed yourself quite out of the coffee-house."

Macaulay described Phillips as "a good Whig and a middling poet." He had the honour of bringing into fashion a species of composition which has been called after his name, Namby Pamby.

Mr Buttons died in 1731, and in "The Daily Advertiser" of October 5 of that year the following notice appeared: "On Sunday morning died, after a three days' illness, Mr Buttons, who formerly kept Buttons' Coffee-house in Russell Street, Covent Garden, a very noted house for wits, being the place where the Lion produced the famous Spectators and Tatlers written by the late Mr Secretary Addison, and Sir Richard Steele, Knight, which works will transmit their names with honour to posterity."

With the death of Addison and the retirement of Steele into the country Buttons' gradually declined in favour, and its frequenters migrated to the Bedford and the Shakespeare. The house afterwards became a private residence.

Another notorious house was the "Rose," of much earlier date than the houses already described. The Rose adjoined Drury Lane Theatre, about which appears the following extract from Pepys: "It being twelve o'clock or little more, to the King's Playhouse, where the doors were not yet open; but presently they did open, and we in, and find many people already come in by private ways into the pit, it being the first day of Sir Charles Sedley's new play so long expected, The Mulberry Garden, of whom, being so reputed a wit, all the world do expect great matters. I having sat here awhile, and eat nothing to-day, did slip out, getting a boy to keep my place, and to the Rose Tavern, and there got half a breast of mutton off of the spit, and dined all alone."

That the Rose had an unsavoury reputation appears from these verses:

Not far from thence appears a pendent sign,
Whose bush declares the product of the vine;
Whence to the traveller's sight the full-blown Rose
Its dazzling beauties doth in gold disclose,
And painted faces flock in tally'd clothes.

In the time of Charles II its landlord was named Long. The Treason Club met here at the time of the Revolution to consult with Lord Colchester, Thomas Wharton, and others, and it was decided that the regiment under Lieut.-Colonel Langdale should desert in a body, which it did on a Sunday in November 1688. It is probable that there were two houses named "Rose," both flourishing at the same time in this neighbourhood, as Mr Walford, in his "Old and New London", describes this tavern as situated in Rose Street, off Long Acre. Mr Peter Cunningham does not agree with this theory.

Tom's was situated at No. 17, Russell Street, and was pulled down in 1856. It was named after its landlord, Mr Thomas West, who committed suicide in 1722 by throwing himself out of a second-floor window of this house. As in the case of Wills's, only the upper portion of the premises was used as the coffee-house, the ground floor being occupied by Mr T. Lewis, the bookseller, and original publisher of Pope's Essay on Criticism. The clientele of this establishment was noted for its smartness, and quite a feature of the house was the frequent display of full-dress uniforms and numerous decorations adorning the persons of its illustrious patrons. Among its frequenters were Dr Johnson, Colman the Elder, Smollett and Fielding, and Colley Cibber. In 1764 a club of about 700 members was formed, the subscription being fixed at one guinea. On the list of members appear the names of Garrick, Samuel Foote, Earl Percy, Sir John Fielding, Richard Clive (the great Lord Clive), Sir Fletcher Norton, the Marquis of Granby, the Duke of Northumberland, and Dr Oliver Goldsmith. The number 700 probably means the total number of members on the rolls from first to last; as the club premises were too small to afford room for the presence of more than a small number at one time. It is quite a notable fact that Tom's was the first club where noblemen associated on equal terms with the professional classes.

The coffee-house business was closed in 1814, and the premises were taken over by Mr Till, the numismatist. Upon his death Mr Webster succeeded him in the business, but afterwards removed to Henrietta Street.

Mr Timbs mentions that the club-room snuff-box was quite a celebrated trophy, being made of tortoise-shell, and having on the lid, in relief, the portraits of Charles I and Queen Anne Maria, and the Boscobel Oak, with Charles II hiding in its branches. Tom's was afterwards known as the Caledonian.

At No. 8, Russell Street, lived Tom Davies, actor and bookseller, at whose house Boswell received his first introduction to the great theme of his discourse, Dr Johnson.

Charles Lamb and his sister lived in this street in lodgings at No. 20, over a brazier's shop. They were evidently charmed with their surroundings, for Lamb wrote to Miss Wordsworth in a letter dated November 21, 1817: "We are in *the* individual spot I like best in all this great city; the theatres with all their noises, Covent Garden, dearer to me than any garden of Alcinous, where we are morally sure of the earliest peas and asparagus. Bow St thieves are examined within a few yards of us. Mary had not been here four and twenty hours before she saw a thief. She sits at the window working; and casually throwing out her eyes, she sees a concourse of people coming this way, with a constable to conduct the solemnity. These little incidents agreeably diversify a female life."

Dr John Armstrong, the poet, died here in 1779; and John Evelyn, the diarist, and Carr, Earl of Somerset, were both, at one time of their lives, residents of Russell Street. The latter lived here in 1664 (Church).

Hummum's Hotel and Restaurant, situated in the south-west corner of the street, and overlooking the market, takes its name from an Eastern word, "Hammam," meaning a warm bath, and was the first example of its kind in England. These places were known as "Bagnios," and resembled a modern Turkish bath. In the eighteenth century the bagnios of the metropolis degenerated into resorts of vice. As early as 1701 the place was advertised as follows:

"The Hummums in Covent Garden having for several years past been neglected and abused by those persons that had the care and management of them, whereby several, persons of quality have been disgusted, and have left off coming thither to sweat and bathe as formerly: This is to give notice, that the said Hummums are now in possession of others, who have refitted the same and rectified all those neglects and abuses that were formerly done there, where persons may sweat and bathe in the cleanliest, and be cupped after the newest, manner. There is like-wise provided good lodging for any persons who shall desire to lodge there all night, where who pleases may see the same. The price, as was always, for sweating and bathing, is 5/6, for two in one room 8/–: but who lodges there all night 10/–."

The Hummums was the scene of Dr Johnson's best accredited ghost story, related by him to Boswell as follows:

"A waiter at the Hummums where Ford, a relation of Johnson's, died, had been absent for some time, and returned not knowing that

Ford was dead. Going down into the cellar, according to the story, he met him. Going down again he met him a second time. When he came up, he asked the people of the house what Ford could be doing there. The waiter took a fever, in which he lay for some time. When he recovered, he said he had a message to deliver to some women from Ford, but he was not to say what, or to whom. He walked out, and was followed, but somewhere near St Paul's Church they lost him. He came back and said he had delivered the message, and the women exclaimed, 'Then we are all undone.' Dr Pellet, who was an incredulous man, enquired into the truth of this strange story, and reported that the evidence was irresistible."

The Bedford stood at the north-east corner of the Piazza, on the site of the west end of the Floral Hall yard. The presiding genius here was Foote, who ruled the company in much the same way as Dryden did at Wills's, and Steele at Buttons'.

The history of the Bedford was written in 1751, reaching, twelve years later, its second edition. The author of this history went by the pseudonym of "Genius," and the book was dedicated to "The Most Impudent Man Alive." The volume is nothing more than a skit on some of the best-known frequenters of the house. Its style exhibits the extreme coarseness attendant on most of the literary productions of the eighteenth century. The author tells us that he was prompted "to transmit its ancedotes to that period, when we may reasonably suppose, thro' the natural vicissitude of things, no vestige of it can possibly remain."

The establishment appears to have been frequented by very well-to-do folk. I quote from its pages: "The situation of this place necessarily makes it a convenient assembly for those who frequent the theatres, as well as those who exert their talents to please the public in dramatic performances, and for the same reason it may be looked upon as the centre of gravitation between the Court and the City; the noxious effluvia of St Bride's are here corrected by the genuine Eau de Luce from Pall Mall; and the predominance of ambergrise at St James' is qualified by the wholesome tar of Thames Street. Nor does the conversation receive a less happy effect from this junction; the price of stocks and the lie of the day from the Alley are softened by the 'bon-mot' of Lady Dolabella, which sets every fool at the Duchess of Trifle's rout in a titter; of the duel which this morning was fought between Captain Terrible and Lord Puncto, when both of them were mortally wounded in the *coat*!"

As the souls of some of these fops were essentially bound up with their dandified attire, this seems to be the most suitable spot for them to receive chastisement.

David Garrick was a familiar figure at this house. He was born at Hereford in 1716, and was the third child of a lieutenant of Dragoons of French origin whose parents had escaped to England when the Huguenots were banished from France. According to Mr Percy Fitzgerald, the family name was de la Garrigue, a connection of the Rochefoucauld family.

David was from his early days gifted with an extraordinary sense of wit and repartee, and as a mere boy would amuse an audience of friends with his mimicry and sallies. He was afterwards sent to Rochester to further his studies, and at the age of twenty-two, together with his brother Peter, who had previously served in the Navy, determined to go into the wine trade. The firm was to have branches at London and Lichfield, and David was appointed to look after the former. They had premises in Durham Yard, situated in that part of the Strand which was afterwards named the Adelphi. Foote taunted Garrick "as living in Durham Yard with three quarts of vinegar in his cellar and calling himself a wine merchant."

David was evidently not destined for a commercial career—his heart was never in the business. His greatest friend was Macklin, an actor in the Drury Lane company. The two were almost inseparable, and spent most of their time in the coffee-houses in the company of other Bohemians. It is not surprising that the wine business, so far as the London branch was concerned, was not a success. The appearance of Margaret Woffington on the stage seems to have finally decided him. He immediately fell a victim to the Irish girl, and abandoned business for the stage.

"The Connoisseur" of January 31, 1754, describes the Bedford as being nightly crowded with men of parts. "Almost every one you meet is a polite scholar and a wit. Jokes and bon-mots are echoed from box to box. Every branch of literature is critically examined, and the merit of every production of the press, or performance of the theatres, weighed and determined."

A shilling rubber club was held here, where a quarrel arose between Hogarth and Churchill, which drew from Walpole the remark that "never did two angry men of their ability throw mud with less dexterity." Mr Wheatley says that the club was closed in 1867. Its effects, sold at Christie's, realised £650.

Hogarth was also a member of a club which held its meetings at the Bedford and joined in a party for a jaunt in Kent, something after the style of Mr Pickwick. Whilst at Rochester, Hogarth and Scott (another member) played at hop-scotch in the Colonnade under the Town Hall.

When Covent Garden Theatre was burnt down, the Bedford and Shakespeare Taverns were saved from destruction by a wall that had been recently erected by the proprietors of the theatre, to guard themselves from fire in that direction.

The Piazza Coffee-house occupied part of the site where now stands the Tavistock Hotel. The proprietor was Macklin, who presided over the coffee-room, and who kept what Fielding described as a "temple of luxury."

In his "Voyage to Lisbon" Fielding writes: "Unfortunately for the fishmongers of London, the Dory resides only in the Devonshire seas; for could any of this company but convey one to the temple of luxury under the Piazza, where Macklin, the high-priest, daily serves up his rich offerings, great would be the reward of that fishmonger."

The Shakespeare Tavern adjoined the Piazza Coffee-house.

The aspect of Russell Street to-day is very different from that which it presented in its palmy days. Many of its houses on the north side have been removed to afford room for the extension of the market. The Hummums has been entirely rebuilt. The site of Wills's (a very old building) was, until recent years, occupied as a ham-and-beef shop, where, contrary to the custom of a restaurant, cooked meat was sold to be eaten not on, but off the premises. Mr Callow, in his "Old London Taverns", says "there are many such shops in London, but few, probably, who do so large a trade as this." The premises have now become an emporium for the sale of bananas and other fruits.

A few old houses still lend to this street something of its ancient aspect, though further alterations and improvements are frequently occurring. The most recent change is seen in the new extension of the Flower Market on the south side. Something in the nature of an old landmark which has now disappeared is "Hooper's Pharmacy," about which the following tale is told. A certain salesman in the market, devoted to practical joking and known to back horses, was one day accosted by a costermonger client, who tried very hard to discover the source of the salesman's turf information. The joker told him that the manager at "Hooper's" was known to make bets, and that, by going about it the right way, the costermonger might possibly get "in the know." He accordingly called on the chemist, and, being asked what he wanted, ordered the first thing that came into his head, to wit, a seidlitz powder. He swallowed the draught, and proceeded to pump the manager. Gaining nothing by his efforts on so barren a soil, he became abusive and would not leave the shop until assisted thereto by a policeman. Whether he afterwards had it out with his friend the salesman, history does not repeat.

Until 1859 the west part of Russell Street from Bow Street to the market was known as Great Russell Street, while the portion running from Bow Street to Drury Lane was called Little Russell Street.

In the latter street and close to Crown Court was a tavern called the "Harp," a resort of long standing of famous actors. Mr Walford, in his "Old and New London", writes that a celebrated society or club called the "City of Lushington" was held here, the members of which were presided over by a "Lord Mayor" and four "Aldermen," each of them elected to their exalted positions. Each member had his particular seat, known as a "ward." The "Edmund Kean corner" was strictly maintained as the seat of honour. The proceedings appear to have been conducted with the greatest decorum and propriety, and not, as the name might seem to suggest, with scenes of drunkenness and levity. The side of Little Russell Street on which this tavern was situated has now entirely disappeared.

Mention must also be made of the "Albion," which was situated in Little Russell Street next door to Hooper's Pharmacy. This was a tavern of some considerable repute in the 'sixties, but must not be confounded with an hotel of the same name in Aldersgate Street, E.C., which was one of the most celebrated hotels in the City.

VII

Bow Street and Wellington Street—Sir Walter Scott—Celebrated inhabitants—The Cock Tavern and riot—Wycherley: his marriage—Dr John Radcliffe: his eccentricities—The old and modern police-stations—The Metropolitan Police Force—Charlotte Clarke—Lawlessness of the streets—Execution in Bow Street—Sir John Fielding, the first stipendiary magistrate—Crown Court and the Scottish Church—Broad Court—Macklin and Mrs Woffington—The Wrekin—Hart Street (now Floral Street)

Bow Street was constructed in 1637, and has been described by Strype as "running in the shape of a bent bow," from which shape it took its name. He also described it as being "open and large, with very good houses, well inhabited, and resorted unto by gentry for lodgings, as are most of the other streets in this parish." Bow Street did not originally connect Long Acre with the Strand; in order to gain access to the latter thoroughfare it was necessary to pass down Brydges Street, now renamed Catherine Street. The street that received the name of Wellington Street in 1844 was originally Charles Street, so named after Charles I. Here Barton Booth, the actor who sustained the role of the original Cato in Addison's play of that name, died in 1733.

It is difficult to believe that Bow Street was once a fashionable locality; yet Dryden, in his epilogue of "King Arthur", wrote the following words, which were spoken by Mrs Bracegirdle, "From fops and wits and cits and Bow Street beaux," etc. Sir W. Scott once remarked that a letter from Bow Street in his day would have been more alarming than otherwise, which shows that the then most important building in the street was the police office. Reference is made to this later. The narrow part of the street between Long Acre and Floral Street was once named Bow Court. At the corner of Broad Court is a branch of the London City & Midland Bank, over which are the offices of Messrs. Garcia, Jacobs & Co., fruit brokers. At No. 8 Bow Street a tobacconist's shop, kept by a Mr Harris, the boundaries of St Paul's, Covent Garden, and St Martin's-in-the-Fields adjoin, this house being situated partially in both parishes.

Robert Harley, the great minister, afterwards created Earl of Oxford, was born here in 1661; and Fielding, the novelist, occupied the house in this street on whose site was subsequently erected the first Bow Street police-station. Here he wrote "Tom Jones." On the east side was the Cock Tavern, kept by a woman known as Oxford Kate. It was here that a disgraceful riot occurred, caused by the disorderly conduct of Sir Charles Sedley, Bart., Lord Buckhurst, and Sir Thomas Ogle, who stripped and exposed themselves in indecent postures to the passers-by. Their conduct so incensed the crowd that a determined attack was made upon the place. The authors of the disturbance were tried before Lord Chief Justice Foster of the King's Bench. Pepys states that "His Lordship and the rest of the Bench did all of them roundly give him a most high reproof; my Lord Chief Justice saying that it was for him and such wicked wretches as he was, that God's anger and judgments hung over us—calling him Sirrah! many times. It seems that they have bound him to his good behaviour, (there being no law against him for it,) for £5,000."

Another writer states he was fined £500, and that Sedley, together with the other culprits, employed Killigrew and another courtier to intercede with the King for a mitigation of the sentence. Tradition, however, relates that, instead of exerting themselves on behalf of their friends, these latter actually begged the amount for their own use, and extorted it to the last halfpenny.

Sedley was the author of several plays, and was also the father of the Countess of Dorchester, mistress of James II.

Opposite the Cock lived Richard, Earl of Dorset, and also Wycherley, the dramatist. Charles II visited the latter here, and, finding him in ill-health, advised him to go abroad, furnishing him with a sum of money for that purpose. Wycherley followed the King's advice. On his return his peregrinations led him to Tunbridge Wells, where he met, fell in love with, and married the young Countess of Drogheda. He failed, however, to acquaint the King of these steps, and his Majesty was seriously offended thereat. Knowing that the countess was the King's ward, Wycherley probably feared that he would not be allowed to marry her, and therefore kept the whole matter a secret. He did not, however, reap much happiness from his bargain, for his wife turned out to be a very jealous woman. She could not bear her husband to be out of her sight; and it is related that when he went to his favourite haunt, the Cock, on the opposite side of the street, he was obliged to leave open the windows of the room in which he sat, that she might see there were no women in his company.

In the reigns of Anne and William III there lived in Bow Street, in a house which stood on the site of the east end of the Floral Hall, the eccentric, though eminent, physician Dr Radcliffe. His eccentricity was accompanied by a bluffness of speech which occasionally brought upon his head the keen displeasure of both his Royal patients. A few years before William's death the Doctor was summoned to attend his Majesty. The King pointed out a curious feature of his malady, viz. the abnormal swelling of the lower limbs, while the rest of the body retained its ordinary dimensions. The Doctor, having made his examination, exclaimed with more force than courtesy, "I would not have your Majesty's two legs for your three kingdoms." William never forgave him for this brusque speech, although he continued to make use of his prescription until a year or so previous to his demise; but he could never again be persuaded to admit the Doctor to his presence.

His remark to Anne, then Princess of Denmark, was equally unfortunate. He treated her illness with great coolness, and remarked that "she has only the vapours, and is as well as any woman breathing, if she could only be persuaded to believe it." When he next appeared at Court he was met by an officer of the Household, who informed him that the Princess no longer had any need of his services. Later on, when her husband was ill, she overcame her former indignation and summoned him to her presence. He was also sent for when she herself lay at death's door. The Doctor disobeyed the summons, pleading illness as an excuse. He was disbelieved, and his callousness aroused great indignation. In one of his letters he writes: "I know the nature of attending crowned heads in their last moments too well to be fond of waiting on them without being sent for by a proper authority." And, again: "You have heard of pardons being signed for physicians before a Sovereign's demise; however, ill as I was, I would have gone to the Queen in a horse-litter had either her Majesty, or those in commission next to her, commanded me to do so."

He therefore appears to have had some grounds for absenting himself, although evidently he could never forget the insult put upon him by the message that the Princess no longer had any need of his services.

He afterwards removed to Great Queen Street, and ultimately to No. 5, Bloomsbury Square, where he died in 1714. He left his books and a large sum of money to the University of Oxford, and thus founded the library there which bears his name (Clinch's "Bloomsbury and St Giles").

Among the celebrated residents of Bow Street were Edmund Waller, the poet, who lived in a house on the east side, where, in 1654, he wrote the celebrated panegyric on Cromwell; William Longueville, friend of Butler; Marcellus Laroone, who drew Tempest's "Cries of London," and lived on the west side from 1680 to 1702; Mohun, the actor, on the east side from 1671 to 1676; and Grinling Gibbons, the wood-carver. The house of the latter fell down in 1710, luckily without injury to the inmates, although a little girl, who was playing in the neighbouring court, was buried in the débris, and killed. "Sir Roger de Coverley" is located here in "Spectator," No. 410; and the Earl of Dorset lived on the west side 1684–5.

Bow Street is to-day celebrated for its Police Court, which is the third example of its kind erected in this particular thoroughfare. The first police court was the original house of the Fieldings, situated on the east side of the street on the site of the premises now occupied by the Opera Hotel and Messrs. Lyons' tea shop. Here Sir John Fielding, the blind magistrate, dispensed justice, in spite of his affliction, until 1790, when his house was destroyed during the "Gordon Riots." It was rebuilt, and served its purpose for some time, but a new edifice was constructed on the opposite side of the road in 1825, on the site of an old tavern known as the Brown Bear. The last case was tried here in 1881. This is without doubt the old building referred to by Dickens in "Oliver Twist". "Antiquarians," writes Mr Sala, "of the type of Whitelocke and Howell, of Strype and Aubrey, and of Pepys and Stow, and above all of old Peter Cunningham, will hereafter take note of a naughty little boy named Patrick McCarthy, who has stolen some logs. His offence is petty; and yet Master McCarthy is the last prisoner who has been put at the bar of the old Bow Street Police Court. To-day we may remind our readers that the old Bow Street offices are closed finally, and henceforth the business will be transacted in the new block of buildings on the opposite side of the street. Indeed the conditions of the old police court had long become a public scandal. It had changed little, if at all, since Dickens described it in "Oliver Twist" and dwelt upon the general air of greasiness and of dirt which hung about it and which seemed more or less to choke and to stifle the faculties and perceptions of all who were engaged in its business, from the Chief Magistrate himself down to the door-keeper. It was, in truth, an evil old place, and it is therefore perhaps pleasant to know that it will soon be swept away."

When this building was finally closed for police purposes in 1881 the court-room was let for a short time to the well-known firm of fruit-brokers, Messrs. Garcia, Jacobs & Co., in which to conduct their sales. It is related by one of the present members of the firm that the buyers were so tickled at the novelty of their surroundings that they insisted upon holding a mock trial, one of their number acting the part of prisoner, and the remainder constituting them-selves counsel, solicitors, jurymen, etc. The auctioneer was naturally the judge (with his natural tendency to "knock down" in abeyance for the time, it is to be hoped), and it was not until after the case had been heard and judgment pronounced that the sale was allowed to proceed.

The police station was on the site of the original police court, on the east side of the street, and when the old building was pulled down, an article appeared in one of the morning papers which described the old place as follows:

"The old charge-room is now filled with lumber; the dock, in which the prisoners stood, has now disappeared; the cells, as black as night, where each iron-lined cell door is covered with rust, are not yet demol-ished. Gaoler White, going over them yesterday with a reporter, saw some rusty keys hanging to an old gas-bracket. He exclaimed, 'Ah! here are the old keys,' and told how, in the good old times, when Seven Dials was Seven Dials, and Drury Lane, Drury Lane, he had seen in the passage adjoining these old cells as many as a dozen men, on a Saturday night, waiting for the doctor to stitch up the wounds sustained in one of the many riots which took place in that district, when he was a young constable. 'Many a time,' said he, 'I and others have had to take the boots from men who were kicking the doors, and keeping the other prisoners awake.'"

The old Bow Street officers were familiarly known as Robin Redbreasts, on account of their wearing red waistcoats. Another name by which they were known was "Runners." As "Scarlet Runners" in pursuit of criminals it may confidently be asserted that they sometimes gave them "beans"!

Before the existence of the Metropolitan Police Force, night watchmen were employed to patrol the streets. The picture that Shakespeare has drawn us of Dogberry and Verges is sufficient to show us how totally unfit for their onerous duties these men were. They were known as the "Watch" and "Charleys." The streets of the town were exceedingly narrow and ill-paved, and abounded, after dark, with dangers to peaceable citizens. Cut-throats and footpads were to be found everywhere, and a man's life was of little value if he chanced to fall into their hands. In seventeenth- and eighteenth-century literature frequent mention is made of the "Mohocks," or bands of armed bullies, who were the terror of the town. These ruffians were kith and kin of our modern Hooligan, with the exception that the Mohocks were chiefly composed of swaggering, boasting individuals, known as "rakes" and "bloods."

Mr Justin McCarthy thinks that the name Mohock was taken from the Mohawk tribe of Indians, which at one time inhabited the site of New York City. The chief sport of these bullies was the watch; and the *modus operandi* was to commence by overturning a "box" with the watchman inside, and afterwards belabouring him soundly with the flat of their swords. Nor did women escape more easily; on the contrary, they generally suffered more than the men. In the time of Queen Anne the lawlessness of the streets reached such a climax that she issued a royal proclamation, promising a reward to any one who would give evidence leading to the arrest of any person found guilty of robbery and outrage.

It must be remembered that London at that period was very different in size from what it is to-day. The district which is the subject of this book, together with Leicester, Soho, and Golden Squares, formed the western boundary of the metropolis, and such districts as are now reckoned part of Central London were then separated from the town by fields and open country. It is therefore not surprising that such a state of violence existed in the streets. The knowledge that no serious check was brought to bear upon it seems to have acted as an incentive to further outrages and deeds of violence. Bribery, moreover, and corruption were rampant, and it was only the poor wretched creatures who were punished, in most instances for little trifling misdemeanours, while My Lord, who had run a man through the body in some drunken frolic, was, by the aid of plenty of coin, allowed to go free, and the matter hushed up.

Mr Knight relates how Charlotte Charke, the eccentric daughter of Colley Cibber, who used to dress as a man, and in the course of her chequered career acted as waiter, somewhere about 1746, at a tavern in Marylebone, then a very thinly populated district standing by itself, used to walk nightly from her place of employment to her residence in or near Long Acre. She writes in her autobiography: "I begged not to be obliged to lie in the house, but constantly came to my time, and stayed till about ten or eleven at night, and I have oft wondered I have escaped without wounds or blows from the gentlemen of the pad, who are numerous and frequent in their evening patrols through the fields; and my march extended as far as Long Acre, by which means I was obliged to pass through the thickest of them."

She evidently refers to the district of St Giles, which was always a dangerous vicinity even in recent years, until the notorious rookeries were swept away, and the neighbourhood cleansed of its unruly denizens.

An article in the "London Mercury" of January 13, 1721, states that there were twenty-two gaming houses in the parish of St Paul, Covent Garden.

A "Presentment" by the Grand Jury of Middlesex, dated 1744, is directed against luxury, extravagance, and vice, and it names persons as well as places: "We, the Grand Jury, sworn to enquire for Our Sovereign Lord, the King, and the body of this county, have observed from most of the presentments of returns delivered to us by the constables of this county, that they have been, as we apprehend and fear, very remiss in their duty, by returning their several districts and divisions to be quiet and in good order, or to that effect.

"Whereas the contrary does most manifestly appear, in many instances as well from the accounts or advertisements we read in the daily papers, printed and dispersed within this county, inviting and seducing not only the inhabitants, but all other persons, to several places kept apart for the encouragement of luxury, extravagance and idleness and, we fear, other wicked and illegal purposes.

"And we do accordingly hereby present, as places riotous, of great extravagance, luxury and idleness and ill fame, the several houses, places and persons following, within this county, to wit;

"1. The Lady Mornington and her gaming-house in or near Covent Garden within this county.

"2. The Lady Castle and her gaming-house, etc.

"3. The proprietors of the avenues leading to and from the leading playhouses in Covent Garden and Drury Lane, in this county, for not preventing wicked, loose and disorderly persons from loiter in the front of their several houses on play-nights; by which neglect and the riotous behaviour of such disorderly persons, many of His Majesty's good subjects are often in danger of losing their lives or receiving some other bodily harm and are frequently robbed of their watches and money, to the great discredit of civil government."

In this year the Lord Mayor and Aldermen presented an address to the King on the confederation of rogues, robbers, and murderers in streets, and their defiance of authority. An Act was passed for the improvement of the lighting in the streets of the City.

Things went from bad to worse, and Shenstone, writing in 1774 about the dangers of the streets, says: "London is really dangerous at this time; the pick-pockets, formerly content with mere filching, make no scruple to knock people down with bludgeons in Fleet Street and the Strand, and that at no later hour than eight o'clock at night; but in the Piazzas in Covent Garden they come in large bodies, armed with couteaux, and attack whole parties, so that the danger of coming out of the playhouse is of some weight in the opposite scale, when I am disposed to go to them oftener than I ought."

In such a state of affairs it is not surprising that no mercy was shown to a criminal when caught. The chief punishment of the day was hanging. Men were hanged then with little regard to the sanctity of human life, and this legal butchery continued till a date very nearly preceding the ascension of Queen Victoria to the throne. The late Lord Brampton (better known as Sir Henry Hawkins) relates, in his "Reminiscences," how a youth of seventeen was hanged at Bedford in 1830 for the terrible crime of setting fire to a hayrick! As they were not particular where they erected the gallows, executions were held in all parts of the town. Tyburn was the chief place of execution, but in 1687 a soldier named William Grant was hanged in the Market for desertion, and in 1760 one Patrick McCarthy was hanged at the foot of Bow Street, Covent Garden. In George IV's time over 200 offences, many of them of the most trivial description, were punishable by death. For many years the humane law student and reformer, Romilly, had endeavoured to amend the criminal laws, but he was continually opposed by Eldon and the rest of the Tories, and it was not until 1823 that Sir R. Peel successfully took up the matter. By his instrumentality the Metropolitan Police Act was passed. This did away with the old Bow Street patrol and the ancient parochial city watch. In their place was substituted one force, to be employed in both day and night duty, the whole being placed under the control of the Home Department. In fact "Charley" gave way to "Bobby," now a recognised and honoured institution, whose resourcefulness and never-failing courtesy command the praise of his own countrymen and foreigners alike.

The present buildings were erected in 1881 at a cost of £40,000. The architect was Mr John Taylor, of H.M. Office of Works and Public Buildings. Many celebrated criminals have appeared here.

Martlet Court, which connects Bow Street with Drury Lane, now separates the police court from the new building at present occupied by the London County and Westminster Bank and Messrs. Elders & Fyffes, Ltd., the well-known banana merchants. Here lived Shuter the actor in March 1756, when he advertised his benefit in the "Public Advertiser" of March 8th of that year.

Blushes each spout in Martlet Court,
And Barbican, moth-eaten fort—
And Covent Garden kennels sport
A bright ensanguined drain.
                    (*Rejected Addresses*)

Running parallel with Bow Street, between Broad Court and Russell Street, is Crown Court. Here, until recently, was situated the Scottish Church, long famous on account of the preaching and prophesying of the Rev. John Cumming, its minister from 1832 to 1879. The building was recently pulled down and the services were transferred to Newton Hall, Fetter Lane. The reverend doctor had the honour of preaching before Queen Victoria at Balmoral in 1850 (Timbs). The church has now been rebuilt, and its principal entrance is in Russell Street, facing the stage door of Drury Lane Theatre.

Here was also the Crown Tavern, where "Punch" was first projected.

In Broad Court, which connects Bow Street with Drury Lane, is St John Church. Built in 1850, for 70 years it was known as the Tavistock Proprietary Episcopal Chapel. In 1833 it was made a chapel of ease to the parish of St Martin's. It became a new Vicarage in 1855, when it was consecrated, and dedicated to St John the Evangelist. At the same time there was taken from the parish of St Martin's and assigned to it a district, which has ever since been a distinct parish for ecclesiastical purposes. The building has been entirely renovated. The interior is dark and somewhat gloomy. Among the objects of interest may be noted a fine old Jacobean pulpit, which was originally in the church at Penshurst, in Kent; also a stained-glass window, presented by the Duke of Bedford.

Broad Court was the place where "Miss Snevellicci's papa" ("Nicholas Nickleby") was to be found when in town, or "if not at home, let him be asked for at the stage door" (Dickens's "London," by Pemberton).

In 1742 Macklin, together with Garrick and Mrs Woffington, lived in a house built by Wilkes the actor, familiarly know as "Gentleman Wilkes." This house was situated next door but one to the theatre. The talented boarders took it in turn to keep house, probably for the sake of economy; and it was here that Dr. Johnson heard Garrick blame Mrs Woffington for her extravagance in having prepared the tea "as red as blood." Spranger Barry, the actor, afterwards lived in this house in 1749.

In 1762 an exhibition of sign-boards was held at Bonnell Thornton's rooms in a house in the upper part of Bow Street, which was a skit on the newly introduced exhibition by the Society of Arts, Manufactures, and Commerce. Hogarth was an exhibitor, "that photograph who flattereth not," as C.S. Calverley calls him. The majority of the paintings were most grotesque, and, for the most part, caricatures on celebrities.

Opposite the theatre, or, to be more precise, at the corner of Broad Court, was a hostel, which, although quite unpretentious in its exterior appearance, enjoyed for a great number of years a certain amount of fame and prosperity. Its proximity to the "joyous neighbourhood" rendered it most convenient to those who were unable to find accommodation elsewhere, and, as it was properly looked after, it became well patronised. The original landlord was named Powell, a native of Shropshire, who named his house the "Wrekin," after a hill situated near his native place. The chief patrons were actors and their friends, and it is said that only wine was supplied to those who entered the coffee-room; hence it appears that the company was very select. Two clubs were located here—"The Rationals" and "The House of Uncommons." We are told that "the tavern shared the fortunes and misfortunes of the theatre; each change of management at the one house was followed by one at the other" (Walford's "London").

A club named the "Mulberries" also met here in 1824. Its chief regulation was the compulsory contribution by each member of a paper bearing upon Shakespeare. It was frequented by Douglas Jerrold, William Godwin, Laman Blanchard, Kenny Meadows, Elton the actor, and Chatfield the artist. Some time afterwards the name of the club was changed to the "Shakespeare," and was joined by Charles Dickens, Justice Talfourd, Maclise, Macready, Frank Stone, etc. (Timbs's "Curiosities of London").

Another tavern of some renown was the "Garrick's Head," which was situated immediately opposite the Covent Garden Theatre, on the site of the present police court. It was here that the notorious Judge and Jury Society met, presided over by Nicholson, the editor of the "Town." Its advertisement ran as follows on the next page:

GARRICK'S HEAD,
BOW STREET.
Exactly opposite the Grand Entrance to the
ROYAL ITALIAN OPERA.

Listen! Ye nocturnal Wanderers in pursuit of joyous hours after the turmoils of industrious daylight! Come and sup at THE GARRICK'S HEAD.

NICHOLSON
has come back, and so has
THE GRIDIRON!
THE JUDGE AND THE JURY SOCIETY at nine o'clock, after which the Lord Chief Baron departs from judicial dignity to become the chairman of the lively board! Give him a look in! SUCH SINGING BY OLD AND NEW FAVOURITES!

Will you go in, Bob? Yes. So will I,
And the old Baron's Gridiron try;
A Chop or Kidney at this hour,
With Pratee like a ball of flour,
Or Steak upon his Lordship's plan
Will renovate the inward man;
A Sausage, Tripe, or Toasted Cheese,
Stout, Ale, or Water, which you please;
And after that upstairs repair
To see the Baron in his chair
To here the lively Song and Joke,
A Glass of Grog, and have a Smoke.
Come from Casino's mazy thread,
To supper at the GARRICK'S HEAD!

MR NICHOLSON begs to solicit attention to the fact that the Front Coffee-room of the Establishment is a Public Supper Room for Ladies and Gentlemen. The most elegant PRIVATE DINING AND SUPPER APARTMENTS upstairs for large or small parties visiting the theatre.

The Lord Chief Baron Nicholson politely reminds his Friends and Patrons of the great accommodation offered in this splendid establishment. Excellent Bed Chambers 1s. 6d. Breakfast, with eggs, or a Rasher of Bacon 1s. 3d. Dinners and Nic-Nacks from 1 o'clock. A hot joint always at six. The Lord Chief Baron presiding, charge 1s. 6d.

Hart Street, running along the north side of the theatre, connects Bow Street with James Street and continues straight through to Garrick Street. It was built in 1637, and took its name either from the White Hart Inn,[1] which is referred to in the Cecil lease in the early chapters of this book, or an inn situated in the immediate vicinity. In the Savoy Church there is an epitaph on an old vintner of the inn who died in 1586:

Here lieth Humphrey Gosling, of London, vintner,
Of the Whyt Hart of this parish a neghbor
Of virtuous behaviour, a very good archer
And of honest mirth, a very good company keeper,

So well inclyned to poore and rich.
God send more Goslings to be sich.

Joe Haines, the actor, died in this street in 1708. In the "Gentleman's Magazine" of Monday, May 5, 1800, the following item of news appeared: "This morning about seven, as a party of the Guards were conveying to the Savoy two deserters whom they had brought from the country, in passing down James Street, Covent Garden, it was discovered that one of them, William Jackson, had slipped from the handcuffs and was attempting to escape by running down Hart Street. Charles Bexton, one of the Guards, immediately fired, and the fugitive fell dead. The ball penetrated the back part of the neck and came out at the side of the mouth. The body, after lying a considerable time in Hart Street, was conveyed to Covent Garden watch-house.[2] The deceased was by birth an Irishman, twenty-two years old, and had lately deserted from the Cornish Fusiliers. A master baker in that neighbourhood had very nearly received the shot; as he, and others, were passing close by the deserter at the moment and heard no alarm until they saw the man drop dead, who had not run six yards from his guard."

Hart Street has been renamed Floral Street, probably on account of its proximity to the Floral Hall. Almost all its shops are now occupied by fruit salesmen.

1. See Appendix.
2. Covent Garden watch-house was situated close by St Paul's Church.

VIII

Covent Garden Theatre and the Floral Hall

Covent Garden Theatre, or the Royal Opera House as it is now often called, was built by John Rich, the proprietor of the Theatre Royal, Lincoln's Inn Fields, on land leased from the Duke of Bedford at £100 per annum ground rent. Thinking that there was, even in those days, room in London for another playhouse, Rich issued a prospectus to the general public inviting them to take shares in the new venture to the extent of one-fiftieth part apiece; the price of each fiftieth to be £300, payable in three instalments of £100 each. This prospectus was issued in December 1730, and was received with so much enthusiasm that by the end of the following month, January 1731, the large amount of £6,000 was subscribed, and the building operations commenced.

An unfortunate accident somewhat delayed the work, which was being rapidly pushed forward. The press accounts of what actually happened vary in their descriptions of it. Either one of the rafters broke loose from the tackle used for lifting it to its position in the roof, or else a portion of the roof itself collapsed. Anyhow, the work was seriously delayed by the occurrence, inasmuch as it was found impossible to complete the building by the end of that year, according to the undertaking made to Rich. In consequence he reopened his show at the Lincoln's Inn Fields house for a short period.

So nervous was Rich lest any further hitch should occur to prejudice his undertaking in any way that he is said to have postponed the date of the opening night, when it became due. A further contributory cause of nervousness was, no doubt, the animosity exhibited towards his new venture by the proprietors of the older theatre in Drury Lane.

He may have thought it desirable, under the circumstances, to leave nothing to chance, and to make sure that everything was in thorough working order before raising the curtain for the first time.

The scenery was painted by Lambert, and the ceiling by Signor Amiconi, who had also painted Lord Tankerville's staircase in his house in St James's Square. The theatre opened with a revival of Congreve's "Way of the World." The house was calculated to hold £200, but, for some reason or other, the takings on the first night only amounted to £115.

The original theatre stood behind some of the houses in Bow Street, and one entrance was approached by a narrow passage running between two of the houses in this street; another was in Hart (now Floral) Street. The grand entrance was under the Piazza, in the north-east corner, on the site of the Piazza entrance to the Floral Hall. It was not until after the theatre was destroyed by fire and rebuilt that the principal entrance was in Bow Street.

There can be no doubt that a place of entertainment of considerable repute existed in Bow Street for many years previous to the erection of the Opera Rouse. In 1690 Mr Franks held a concert of vocal and instrumental music at the Two Golden Balls at the upper end of Bow Street. In February 1691 this entertainer had removed next "Bedfordgate" in Charles Street (now Wellington Street). In 1718 (at a period when lesser stars had to compete with the combination of musical talent, leading names, and an occasional novelty of an Italian singer, usually brought forward at Stationers' Hall, at York Buildings, and other places of attraction), we find a concert at the Golden Balls in Hart Street at the upper end of Bow Street. There was also one advertised for the entertainment of the Prince Eugène in 1712.

Whether this place of public resort was afterwards razed to the ground and the site formed any part of that used for the theatre is uncertain. Mr Richardson of the Piazza Coffee-house was in possession of a ticket on which were the words, "For the Musick at the Playhouse in Covent Garden, Tuesday, March 6th, 1704. (J.T. Smith's additional plates to the "Antiquities of Westminster.")

This ticket might have either referred to Punch's Theatre under the Little Piazza or to the concert already described, and even to Drury Lane Theatre, although the latter was generally described as being in Brydges Street, Covent Garden.

The first season at Covent Garden may be considered satisfactory. One great advantage which the new house enjoyed over its neighbour, Drury Lane, lay in the position of the royal box, which in the latter house was so situated as to oblige the lords and ladies in attendance to cross the stage to gain access to it—a practice which was naturally found objectionable in many ways. The royal box at Covent Garden, on the other hand, was easily approached—which improvement was not only much appreciated, but served not a little to attract royal patronage.

In the second season the theatre was taken for the performance of the oratorios of Handel, who, a few years later, proposed a scheme of Italian opera for London, towards the floating of which the large amount of £50,000 was subscribed. Handel was entrusted with the task of finding the singers; but it does not appear that the speculation was successful, although a few operas were performed.

In 1735 the celebrated "Sublime Society of Beefsteaks" was formed in the theatre, a coterie of the best-known men of the period, founded by Rich. The latter was a jovial, witty individual, into whose room dropped many an eminent man to enjoy a chat with him and his scene-painter, Lambert. After a talk, pleasant and entertaining, "de omnibus rebus et quibusdam allis," the visitor was induced to remain and help to demolish a steak, which the two worthies used to prepare for their dinner on a stove in the room. This juicy fare, accompanied by a bottle of the best port procured "from the tavern close by," and eaten in such jovial company, proved a great attraction. The fame thereof was soon noised abroad, and others joined and founded that convivial assembly which lasted for a period of 132 years.

The original list of members was limited to twenty-four, amongst whom figure the names of Rich, Lambert, Hogarth, Ryan, Robert Scott, and John Thornhill. Mr Walter Arnold, who has written the history of the Society, denies the statement, which has frequently appeared in print, that the list of the twenty-four members was ever extended to admit George IV, when Prince of Wales. In fact he states that, although his Royal Highness had expressed his desire to join, he had to wait his turn until a vacancy occurred. Those who succeeded the original members were the Earl of Sandwich, George Coleman, Wilkes, John Beard the singer, the Earls of Surrey and Effingham, John Kemble, the Prince of Wales, and the Duke of York.

The Society existed in its original locality until the destruction of

the theatre by fire in 1808, when it moved to temporary quarters at
the Bedford Coffee-house in the Piazza, before moving to the Lyceum
Theatre. The latter move took place in the following year, the management of Covent Garden refusing to allow the Club to meet in the
theatre as of old. The Society had its headquarters at the Lyceum until
1830, when the house was burnt down. It then met at the Lyceum
Tavern close by in the Strand. After shifting its quarters to the Bedford
again for a period of eight years, it finally removed once more to the
Lyceum. At one time the members arrayed themselves in a uniform
consisting of a blue coat and buff waistcoat with brass buttons bearing a gridiron, and the motto, "Beef and Liberty." The curious may
consider the other concomitants of Liberty as exhibited in the cries
(or mottoes) "Wilkes and Liberty," "Imperium et Libertas," "Liberty,
Equality, and Fraternity"; and may reflect that Liberty, at any rate, has
been offered in her time a varied choice of bedfellows.

There have been other clubs of this name, one of which, founded
by Estcourt the actor, included Peg Woffington among its members.
Another one, in existence in 1733, displayed keen hostility to Sir Robert
Walpole.

To resume the history of the theatre: the competition to obtain the
best talent became very strong between Covent Garden and Drury
Lane. Garrick, who was creating an enormous sensation at Goodman's
Fields Theatre, quite "drew the town," with disastrous results to the box
offices of the other houses. Things reached a climax when Fleetwood,
the manager of Drury Lane, secured the services of the new "star" at
the salary, then unheard-of, of six hundred guineas. Rich retaliated
by engaging next season the most talented and popular actress of her
time, Mrs Cibber, who played Desdemona to Quin's Othello. The
next celebrated actress who trod the boards of Covent Garden Theatre
was Mrs Clive.

In 1808 occurred the disastrous fire. This calamity has been attributed to a piece of smouldering wadding, fired from a gun during the
course of the play, "Pizarro," which was being acted on that fateful
evening. The fire, as far as can be ascertained, began at about four
o'clock in the morning, and in the course of two hours the place was
gutted. A number of firemen lost their lives by the fall of a part of the
roof. Of the eleven houses in Bow Street fronting the theatre, seven
were burnt to the ground, including a tavern called the "Smugglers."
The fire destroyed Handel's organ, which he bequeathed to Rich, the

wardrobe of dresses and properties, the wines of the Beef steak Club, and, what was more important, the library of original MS. scores of operas. So strong was the sympathy felt for Kemble that a subscription list, most liberally supported, for funds to rebuild the theatre was at once started. The Duke of Northumberland offered Kemble £10,000, which he would only accept as a loan. The Duke, however, when the foundation-stone of the new theatre was laid, returned the bond, with the message that he hoped it would go to the bonfire which he presumed would celebrate the joyful event.

The first stone of the new structure was laid by the Prince of Wales, who had headed the subscription list with £1,000, with full Masonic honours on December 30, 1808, and it is to be remarked that Kemble on the previous evening was initiated into the mysteries of ancient Freemasonry. The architect was R. Smirke, jun., afterwards Sir Richard Smirke, who also designed the Mint, General Post Office, and the British Museum.

It may be observed, before leaving the subject, that this was not the only theatre whose destruction was due to the firing of a gun on the stage. One of the earliest of our theatres, viz. the Globe at Bankside, at which Shakespeare acted, suffered a like fate from a similar cause. It was built in 1593, and burnt down in 1613 during a performance of "Henry VIII."

The advent of the new theatre was marked by disgraceful scenes of riot and disorder, on account of the raising of the prices which was found necessary because of the enormous expenditure which the rebuilding entailed. Exception was also taken to the private boxes. The disturbances were known as the O.P. (old prices) riots, which continued for seventy-seven nights, in spite of the arrest of many of the ringleaders. The bad feeling appears to have been more particularly manifested against Kemble. Madame Catalini came in for a share of it, apparently because she was a foreigner, on the "heave half a brick at him" principle. Kemble employed pugilists to go into the pit and fight the rioters. For this action, which only increased the trouble, he was forced to apologise before the riots came to an end. The chief ringleader was a certain Henry Clifford; and such was the excitement caused by these disgraceful scenes throughout the town that people were seen wearing the O.P. devices on their hats and coats.

Covent Garden Theatre was again destroyed by fire on March 5, 1856, whilst under the tenancy of J.H. Anderson, "the Wizard of the

North." He had advertised a "carnival benefit," which commenced the Monday afternoon, and continued till midnight. The cast consisted of the united staff of Drury Lane, Strand, and Covent Garden Theatres, and the festivities were to be concluded on the following evening by a *bal masqué*. The fire was discovered while the latter was in progress. It appears that Gye, the then lessee (1849–78), was much opposed to the idea of a ball, and only gave his consent out of consideration for the losses which Anderson had sustained while the theatre was under his tenancy. The fire was discovered at 4.55 a.m., March 5, in the carpenters' room, just as the National Anthem was being played to conclude the entertainment. So fierce were the flames that the roof fell in within an hour of the outbreak.

A report of the fire, describing it as a magnificent spectacle, says: "And now the flames had burst through the roof, and columns of fire dashed into the air, illuminating the surrounding neighbourhood for a distance of three miles, and showing the distant Surrey Hills standing out in bold relief. The glare, visible throughout the entire metropolis, roused the watches at every station throughout the fire brigade, and in a very few minutes the lumbering noise of the engines was heard at the end of Bow Street. Curiously enough, the first engine on the spot was one of those belonging to Messrs. Delafield & Co., a partner of which house had ruined himself in the conduct of the opera" ("Annals of Covent Garden Theatre," by H. Saxe Wyndham). Great crowds were attracted to the scene next day, which included the Queen and Prince Albert, and many other members of the Royal Family. Thus the neighbourhood of Bow Street and the Opera temporarily became again a fashionable promenade. The theatre was rebuilt, and opened as an Italian Opera House in 1858.

The following is a list of some of the principal events connected with the theatre:

1740.	First appearance of Peg Woffington.
1746.	First appearance of David Garrick.
1759.	Last appearance of George Frederic Handel.
1773.	First production of "She Stoops to Conquer."
1786.	First appearance *here* of Mrs Siddons.
1802.	John P. Kemble becomes manager.
1805.	First appearance of Charles Matthews.
1808.	First fire and destruction of theatre.

1809.   O.P. riots on reopening of theatre.

1816.   First appearance *here* of Macready.

1817.   Retirement of J.P. Kemble.

1819.   Last appearance of Mrs Siddons (died 1831).

1837.   Macready manager.

1856.   Theatre again burnt down.

1861.   Début of Adelina Patti.

1888.   Augustus Harris manager. Engagement of Brothers De Reszké and Melba.

1896.   Death of Sir Augustus Harris.

1897.   Royal Syndicate become lessees of the theatre.

1907.   Début of Madame Tetrazzini.

The theatre was also let out for the Anti-Corn-Law meetings in 1843, and here Daniel O'Connell addressed a crowded and enthusiastic meeting on the night that the verdict at the State trial in Dublin was reversed by the writ of error from the House of Lords.

Since the last time the theatre was destroyed until the present day rumour has continually stated that the theatre is to be removed to another quarter. One reason assigned for this is that the Duke of Bedford requires the site for the extension of the Floral Hall. However, threatened men live long, and it would indeed be a pity if the scene of so many triumphs and of such historic interest should be removed to another site.

The theatre looks its best when a gala performance is given on the occasion of some foreign Royal personage visiting the metropolis. On these occasions a guard of honour of one of the Guards Regiments is always posted in Bow Street with the colours and band; and a very interesting spectacle is enjoyed by the Crowds outside the theatre by the arrival of the King and Queen and their guests, whilst the interior is graced with a magnificent display of uniforms and orders of all descriptions, which in conjunction with the beautiful toilettes and jewels of the ladies present a picture of unparalleled splendour.

Immediately adjoining the Opera House is the Floral Hall. This elegant building was intended for a central flower-market, and has been minutely described by Mr Walford in his "Old and New London":

"The ground-plan of the building may be described as resembling two sides of an unequal triangle, the principal entrance being by the side of the new opera house in Bow Street, at the end of the longer side of the figure, while the other opens upon Covent Garden Market, on the side of the Piazza. The public footway of the Piazza is continued along the Covent Garden entrance, in the shape of a gallery roofed with glass and iron. The main arcades run in a direct line from the entrances, and are surmounted at the point of junction by a lofty dome of 50 feet span, which forms an imposing object in the view. This dome, as well as the roofs, are principally composed of wrought iron; the arches, columns, and piers are of cast iron; the frontage, both in Bow Street and the Piazza, is of iron and glass, of which the entire structure is chiefly composed, brickwork forming but a very small part of the composition. The utmost length of the arcade, from the Bow Street entrance to the west wall, is 227 feet; and the length of the shorter side, from Covent Garden Market to the wall of the theatre, nearly 100 feet. The total height, from the ground to the top of the arched dome, is rather over 90 feet. Each of the main arcades is 75 feet wide, and has a side-aisle between the main columns and the wall, 13 feet in width and 30 feet in height. The entrances are both elegant and simple, the doorways being so deeply recessed as, in conjunction with the richly designed iron arches which give admission to the interior, to obviate the flat appearance which generally characterises buildings of glass and iron. The interior is fully equal in lightness and grace of design to the exterior. The columns which support the roof are of cast iron, with richly ornamented capitals, the latter perforated, in order to ventilate the basement beneath, with which the hollow columns communicate. The ground having been excavated beneath, the principal floor forms a basement of the same area as the building above it, and 16 feet in height, the floor of the arcade being supported by cast-iron columns. This building was, as its name implies, designed for a flower-market."

It was opened on March 7, 1860, with a Volunteer ball, under the patronage of Royalty, and for a time was employed for promenade concerts. It was afterwards mad the principal market for those salesmen who had previously been engaged in the sale and distribution of foreign fruit in the market and whose accommodation was insufficient to cope with the fast-increasing qualities of foreign and colonial fruit.

It has been used for this purpose since that date, and it is here that the principal sales are held. The original idea of the flower-market was carried out by the erection of another imposing structure in the south-east part of the market.

IX

*Drury Lane—Craven House—Olympic and Globe
Theatres—Madame Vestris—William, Lord Craven, and
the Thirty Years' War—Terrible condition of Drury Lane
in the seventeenth and eighteenth! centuries—Celebrated
inhabitants of former days—Nell Gwynn—Mrs
Bracegirdle—The Cockpit Theatre—Pepys' notes on its
destruction—Davenant and Betterton—First Drury Lane
Theatre—Theatre in Portugal Row—Burning of Drury
Lane Theatre—Sheridan and the House of Commons—
The present building—Its recent escape from destruction—
Celebrated players at Drury Lane—Playgoing in the
time of Charles II—Present-day scenes—pantomime—
Outbreak of the Great Plague—Vinegar Yard and the
Whistling Oyster—Old burial-ground in Russell Court*

Stow ascribes the name of this thoroughfare to the fact that the
residence of the Drurie, or Drury, family was there situated. Some
authorities are of opinion that this house was built by Sir W. Drury
in the reign of Elizabeth; while Mr Charles Gordon, in his "Old-time
Kingsway and Aldwych and Neighbourhood," states that it was built
generations before this date by a Sir Roger Drury, who died in 1495.

In spite of the difference of opinion as to the original builder, it
is certain that the house existed as a residence. It was situated on
the site of the old Olympic Theatre, and was eventually known as
Craven House, pulled down in 1803. The Olympic Theatre was built
two years later by Philip Astley, and like its neighbour, the Globe,
has now disappeared. It was burnt down on March 29, 1849, but was

reconstructed and re-opened at the end of that year. Cunningham states that the original house was constructed from the timbers of a French warship, the *Ville de Paris*. The masts of the vessel formed the flies, and, when the fire took place, they were seen still erect long after the roof had fallen in. The celebrated Madame Vestris was responsible for much of the success which this theatre enjoyed.

The most celebrated tenant of Craven House was William, Lord Craven, who showed conspicuous bravery at the battle of Creutznach in 1632, during the Thirty Years' War.

Lord Craven was reported to have been secretly married to the widowed Queen of Bohemia, daughter of James I of England, who had formerly married the Elector Palatine. In his interest the Protestant party in Germany had made a Kingdom of Bohemia, in the vain hope that the assistance of James I would enable them to make head against the Catholic Emperor. During the Thirty Years' War Frederic unfortunately lost everything, and on his death his widow sought the protection of Lord Craven, her husband's close friend, who had fought in his cause, and helped to bring up her children (Leigh Hunt). Her Majesty resided at Craven House for some years, and afterwards took up her abode at Leicester House in the Strand, afterwards known as Norfolk House, where she died in 1661.

Lord Craven was always a very active man, renowned for his bustling energy. Whenever a fire broke out in the metropolis, Lord Craven was sure to be one of the first on the scene, mounted on horse back, and giving orders to the soldiers who, in those days, were always summoned to preserve order. It is said that his horse "smelt a fire as soon as it happened."

Drury Lane has been known as Via de Aldwych, and also at one period as Princes Street. It was once inhabited by people of a very good class, but gradually declined into a den of iniquity, and until recent years was considered to be a dangerous locality, adjoining, as it did, the notorious rookery of St Giles. At the close of the seventeenth century it had become a sink of iniquity, in which state it continued for a considerable period. Its courts and alleys were peopled by the lowest dregs of humanity; prostitution and its attendant horrors were allowed to flourish unchecked, until at length the scandal became so great that the authorities were aroused to action, and the neighbourhood was cleansed of its frightful slums. Gay's lines give a vivid description of this pestilential spot:

Oh! may thy virtues guard thee through the roads
Of Drury's mazy courts and dark abodes,
The Harlots' guileful paths, who nightly stand
Where Katherine Street descends into the Strand.
Stay, vagrant Muse, their wiles and subtle arts,
To lure the strangers' unsuspecting hearts
So shall our Youth on healthful sinews tread,
And city cheeks grow warm with rural red.

.   .   .   .   .

'Tis she who nightly strowls with sauntering pace,
No stubborn stays her yielding shape embrace;
Beneath the lamp her tawdry ribbons glare.

.   .   .   .

High-draggled petticoats her travels show,
And hollow cheeks with artful blushes glow;
With flatt'ring sounds she soothes the cred'lous ear,
My noble Captain! Charmer! Love! My Dear!
In riding-hood, near Tavern-doors she plies,
Or muffled pinners hide her livid eyes.

Even before these lines were penned Steele had described the state of affairs in "The Tatler". He wrote in the issue of July 26, 1709:

"There is near Covent Garden a street known by the name of Drury, which, before the days of Christianity, was purchased by the Queen of Paphos, and is the only part of Great Britain where the tenure of her vassalage is still in being. All that long course of buildings is under particular districts or ladyships, after the manner of lordships in other parts, over which matrons of known abilities preside, and have, for the support of their age and infirmities, certain taxes paid out of the rewards of the amorous labours of the young. This seraglio of Great Britain is disposed into convenient alleys and apartments, and every house, from the cellar to the garret, inhabited by nymphs of different orders, that persons of every rank may be accommodated."

Drury Lane, however, was once respectably inhabited. As a proof of this may be cited, in the list of names of former residents, those of Sir William Alexander, Earl of Stirling, the Marquis of Argyll in 1634, Oliver Cromwell in 1646, Lacy, the comedian, 1665–81, the Earl of Anglesea, 1669–86. Here also lived that well-known but frail beauty, Mistress Eleanor Gwynn, who was born at the Coal Yard at the Holborn end of Drury Lane. She afterwards lived in Maypole Alley, since known as Drury Court. It was here that our old friend and gossip, Pepys, saw her looking at the dance going on around the Strand maypole. He writes May 1, 1667: "To Westminster, in the way meeting many milkmaids with their garlands upon their pails, dancing with a fiddler before them; and saw pretty Nelly, standing at her lodging door Drury Lane, in her smock sleeves and bodice, looking upon one: she seemed a mighty pretty creature." Nelly's history is so well known that it would be superfluous to allude to it here any further. Suffice it to say that, in spite of her many failings, she proved a good friend to the poor, and died much regretted.

In Drury Lane the abduction of Mrs Bracegirdle, the actress, was unsuccessfully attempted by Lord Mohun.

The Phœnix, or Cockpit, Theatre, which stood on the site of Cockpit Place, dated back probably to the time of Shakespeare. Whether the building was at one time used as a cockpit is a matter of conjecture; but it was not converted into a playhouse till the reign of James I, when it was raided and destroyed by a Puritan mob on Shrove Tuesday, 1617. The performances were of a very low character, and it was probably on this account that it was attacked.

In the opinion of one writer the destruction was the work of the London apprentices, who claimed a right to demolish houses of ill-fame on Shrove Tuesdays. On March 24, 1667, there was trouble in London with the apprentices for wishing to pull down bad and disorderly houses. Pepys writes:

"Thence back to White Hall: where great talk of the tumult at the other end of the town, about Moore-fields, among the prentices taking the liberty of these holydays to pull down brothels. And, Lord! to see the apprehensions which this did give to all people at Court, that presently order was given for all the soldiers, horse and foot, to be in arms; and forthwith alarmes were beat by drum and trumpet through Westminster, and all to their colours and to horse, as if the French were coming into the town. So Creed, whom I met here, and I to Lincoln's Inn Fields, thinking to have gone into the fields to have seen the prentices; but here we found these fields full of soldiers all in a body, and my Lord Craven commanding of them, and riding up and down to give orders like a madman. And some young men we saw brought by soldiers to White Hall, and overheard others that stood by to say that it was only for pulling down the brothels; but none of the bystanders finding fault with them, but rather of the soldiers for hindering them."

The Cockpit was rebuilt, and existed for some years until it was again attacked. Davenant opened it again in 1656, together with Betterton, until they removed to the theatre in Portugal Row, Lincoln's Inn Fields. The old theatre gradually declined in favour, and was finally vacated; after which Killigrew opened the first Drury Lane Theatre in 1663. It is said that he was joined in his speculation by Mohun, Harte, Dryden, and others. The house was known as the King's House, or Theatre Royal, and was burnt down in 1671–2. The next building was designed by Wren, and was opened on March 26, 1674. It is curious to think that at this period only two theatres were considered necessary for the whole of London, viz. Drury Lane, and Davenant's in Portugal Row.

The two companies at length joined forces, and played together at the new house in 1682. Wren's house was refronted by the Brothers Adam in Garrick's time.

The theatre was rebuilt in 1794, and was described by Mrs Siddons as the "Wilderness," probably on account of its size.

As so many theatres had been destroyed by fire, Mr Holland, the architect of the new building, determined to take every precaution. An iron curtain which resisted the force of a sledge-hammer was constructed so as to let down in a moment of danger, and separate the audience from the stage, while a reservoir was formed at the top of the house, filled with water sufficient, as the epilogue spoken at the opening of the theatre by Miss Farren gave assurance, to "drown the audience in a minute."

On the first night the iron curtain was let down and the stage filled with water, on which a man rowed round in a boat, the managers boasting of their reservoirs—

A firm reliance,
Whose streams set conflagration at defiance.

In spite of these precautions it was totally destroyed by fire on the night of February 24, 1809, in the space of three hours. Its flames lit up the interior of the House of Commons, which was then sitting. On the cause being made known, a motion was made to adjourn; but Sheridan, who was the principal shareholder, seeing that the House was occupied with a serious debate, exclaimed that "whatever might be the extent of the present calamity, he hoped it would not interfere with the public business of the country" (Moore's "Life of Sheridan").

The present building was opened in 1812, the prologue to the entertainment being written by Byron. The portico was erected during the lesseeship of Elliston (1819–26), and the colonnade in Russell Street in 1831. The interior has been greatly altered and enlarged, a portion of the foyer being utilised for the purpose of extending the auditorium, thus providing more seating accommodation.

The house very narrowly escaped destruction in April 1908, but was fortunately saved by the fireproof curtain, with which every theatre is compulsorily equipped, and which was happily more effective than that constructed in 1794. The stage and all the properties and scenery were totally destroyed. The rebuilding was speedily taken in hand, and the new stage is fitted with every modern contrivance for the rapid shifting of scenery, etc.

Among the remarkable events in the history of Drury Lane Theatre was the attempt to assassinate King George III as he was about to enter the royal box on May 15, 1800. The perpetrator of the outrage was a maniac named Hatfield, who was confined in the New Bethlem Hospital. The ball only missed the King by eighteen inches.

Nell Gwynn made her first appearance here in 1666; Booth, 1701; Garrick, 1743; Mrs Siddons, 1775; John P. Kemble, 1783; Edmund Kean, 1814. Macready took leave of the stage here on February 26, 1851.

Mr Leigh Hunt's description of playgoing in the reign of the "merrie monarch" is typical of the customs and manners of that period:

"We now therefore pass Drury House, proceed up the lane by my lord Craven's garden, and turn into Russell Street amongst a crowd of cavaliers in flowing locks and ladies with curls à la Vallière. Some of them are in masks, but others have not put theirs on. We shall see them masking as the house grows full. It is early in the afternoon. … There press a crowd of gallants, who have already got enough wine. Here, as fast as the lumbering coaches of the day can do it, dashes up to the door my lord Duke of Buckingham, bringing with him Buckhurst and Sedley. Then comes a greater though at that time a humbler man, to wit, John Dryden, in a coat of plain drugget, which by and by his fame converted into black velvet. He is somewhat short and stout, with a roundish dimpled face, and a sparkling eye; and, if scandal says true, by his side is 'Madam' Reeves, a beautiful actress, for so the ladies of the stage were entitled at that time. Horses and coaches throng the place, with here and there a sedan; and by the pulling off of hats we find that the King and his brother James have arrived. The former nods to his people as if he anticipated their mutual enjoyment of the play; and the latter affects a graciousness to match, but does not do it very well. As soon as the King passes in, there is a squeeze and a scuffle, and some blood is drawn, and more oaths uttered, from which we hasten to escape. Another scuffle is silenced on the King's entrance, which also makes the gods quiet; otherwise at no period were they so loud. The house is not very large, nor very well appointed. Most of the ladies mask themselves in the pit and boxes, and all parties prepare for a play that shall render it proper for the remainder to do so. The King applauds a new French tune played by the musicians. Gallants, not very sober, are bowing on all sides of us to ladies not very nice; or talking to the orange girls who are ranged in front of the pit with their backs to the stage. We hear criticisms on the last new piece, on the latest panegyric, libel, or new mode. Our friend Pepys listens and looks everywhere, tells all who is who, or asks it and his neighbours think him a most agreeable fat little gentleman. The curtain rises: enter Mistress Marshall, a pretty woman, and speaks a prologue which makes all the ladies hurry on their masks, and convulses the house with laughter. Mr Pepys 'do own' that he cannot help laughing too, and calls the actress a 'merry jade'; but lord, he says, 'to see the difference of the times and but two years ago.'"

How different from this description by Leigh Hunt is the scene presented by Old Drury at the present day! The Drury Lane pantomime is a household word, and a treat anticipated by children for months ahead.

The time to see Old Drury at its best is on Boxing night, when the vast auditorium is filled to its utmost capacity and seats are at a premium. All day long crowds have been waiting at the pit and gallery entrances; some have been there since early morning, but for such enthusiasts the cold has no terror. The crowd is as good-humoured as only a London crowd can be, and, once inside in the warmth, its spirits rise to the occasion. The appearance of Mr "Jimmy" Glover at the conductor's desk is the signal for much cheering. Jimmy is most popular, and has presided over the orchestra for many years. He taps his desk, and the annual overture, consisting of all the popular songs of the year, commences. Pit and gallery join in each well-known air, and in the meantime the house gradually fills, many celebrities being present. In a few minutes the whole audience is upstanding to the strains of the National Anthem. The lights are lowered, and the pantomime, for which Old Drury is so famous, begins its career. At a late hour the audience files out into the cold and deserted streets, paterfamilias doing his utmost to get some sort of conveyance, while mamma and the youngsters wait inside the hall until they are called, the latter with heavy hearts, reflecting that the great treat is at last a *fait accompli*, and unfortunately very conscious of the approaching end of the holidays and the return to school.

In olden times there was some difficulty in gaining access to the theatre. Walker, writing in "The Original" in 1836, says: "Within memory, the principal carriage approach to Old Drury Lane Theatre was through that part of Drury Lane which is now a flagged foot-passage, and called Drury Court, just opposite the new church in the Strand."

It was in this neighbourhood that the great Plague of London first broke out at the latter end of November 1664, when two Frenchmen died of the distemper in Long Acre, or rather at the upper end of Drury Lane (Defoe's Journal of the Plague Year). The large increase in the bills of mortality in this parish during six calendar months caused the public some alarm, although the authorities endeavoured to keep it as secret as possible. Defoe writes: "Few dared to go through Drury Lane and the other streets suspected, unless they had extraordinary business that obliged them to do it." Pepys noted on June 7, 1665[1]: "The hottest day that I ever felt in my life. This day, much against my will, I did in Drury Lane see two or three houses marked with a red cross on the doors, and 'Lord, have mercy on us,' writ there; which was a sad sight to me, being the first of the kind that to my remembrance I ever saw."

Adjoining the theatre there existed, until the recent improvement of the neighbourhood, a maze of courts and alleys giving access one to the other, and inhabited by a heterogeneous rabble who rendered the vicinity dangerous to venture upon. In one of these alleys was a house, which gave admission to another court from the back, and it was reckoned high sport by the denizens to go in at the front door, throw a brick at the policeman when he appeared, and then run out at the back, and so make their escape.

Vinegar Yard, which directly adjoined the theatre, was originally Vine Garden Yard, or Vineyard, and was built about 1621. This court was from the time of its construction little more than a place of bad repute, being no more savoury than the notorious Lewkner's Lane, a street wholly inhabited by prostitutes.

In Vinegar Yard stood a small tavern, or oyster and refreshment rooms, known as "The Whistling Oyster," and, according to Mr Walford, a haunt of Bohemians and artists. The sign of the house was a humorous picture of a gigantic oyster whistling a tune, with a twinkle in its eye. The tale goes that about 1840 the proprietor, when passing a tub filled with delicate "natives," heard a curious (as the French would say) "sifflement." On investigating the cause he found that one of the oysters was actually whistling. Thereupon the fortunate and accomplished performer was removed from the tub full of its less vocally gifted comrades, and placed by itself in a post of honour. The news of this tuneful crustacean (no longer one of the *muti pisces*) spreading, the place was soon besieged by people anxious to view the phenomenon. The consequence was that a roaring (or whistling) trade was done, and the hero of the occasion, like Nero, fiddled (or fifed) whilst Rome burnt. That the oyster did actually whistle is beyond question, the cause being ascribed to the existence of a minute hole in the shell, and the action of breathing probably caused the noise which gave it fame.

Vinegar Yard has now entirely disappeared, with the exception of a very small portion which has been converted into a covered way, in which are situated the pit and gallery entrances to the theatre.

Russell Court, which was close by, was a narrow little alley, at the bottom of which was situated an old burial-ground, surrounded by tumble-down, rickety hovels. It has been stated that this ground was the filthy cemetery described by Dickens in "Bleak House", as "Tom's-all-alone." Others have ascribed the spot in the novel to the old and now covered burial-ground in Drury Lane, recently converted into a recreation ground for the children by the Westminster Council.

"'He was put there,' says Jo, pointing. 'Over yonder. Among them piles of bones, and close to that there kitchen winder. They put him wery nigh the top. They was obliged to stamp on it to get it in. I could unkiver it for you with my broom, if the gate was open. That's why they locks, I s'pose,' giving it a shake, 'It's always locked. Look at that rat,' cries Jo, excited. 'Hi, look, there he goes. Ho! Into the ground.' 'Is this place of abomination consecrated ground?' 'I don't know nothink of consequential ground,' says Jo, still staring. 'Is it blessed?' 'I'm blest if I know,' says Jo, staring, more than ever, 'but I should think it warn't. Blest?' repeats Jo, something troubled in his mind. 'It ain't done much good if it is. Blest? I should think it was t'othered, myself. But I don't know nothink.'"

A story is told of a navvy looking out of a top window of one of the surrounding hovels on a funeral taking place below. When the clergy-man arrived at that part of the service "I heard a voice from Heaven," the navvy called out, "You're a liar; I'm nearer to Heaven than you are, and I can't hear anything."

The site of this place is now directly at the back of the Waldorf Theatre and Hotel, and is paved over. Blocks of workmen's dwellings surround the spot, upon the wall of which a tablet has been erected, thus inscribed:

"A part of the forecourt, as well as the site on which this wall is erected, is a portion of the old burial-ground of the parish of St Mary le Strand, and is vested in the Rector of the said parish. The north and south boundaries of the old burial-ground are indicated by red stones let into the foot pavement.

> "F. HARCOURT HILLESDON, M.A., *Rector*.
> "W.O. READER, *Clerk*.

> *"June 1907."*

1. See Appendix.

X

Catherine Street—Brydges Street—York and Tavistock
Streets—Tavistock Row—Murder of Miss Ray—
Wimbledon House in the Strand—D'Oyley's warehouse—
Gaiety Theatre—"Morning Post"—Lyceum Theatre
and Exeter Change, Wellington Street—The Victoria
Club—"Household Words"—Voltaire—Covent Garden
Hotel—Maiden Lane—Andrew Marvell, Southampton
Street—J.M.W. Turner—The Cider Cellars—Professor
Porson—Rule's—Henrietta Street and its fashionable
inhabitants

Catherine Street, which now connects Russell Street with Aldwych, was at one time the only direct route to the Strand from the neighbourhood of Covent Garden. The upper part of this street, which extended as far as York Street, was called Brydges Street, whilst the lower portion, which reached to the Strand, was named Catherine Street. The former thoroughfare was named after George Brydges, Lord Chandos, and was built about 1637. There were several taverns of note here, viz, the Drury Tavern, the Sir John Falstaff, the Elysium, and the Sheridan Knowles. A club named "The Owls" met at the last-named, of which Sheridan Knowles was a patron and a frequenter. Every panel of the room was inscribed with the name of some dead or living man of letters. Besant states that after the Great Fire, the first post office, which originally stood in Cloak Lane, Downgate Hill, was removed to Brydges Street for a time. In 1690 it was shifted to Lombard Street, and afterwards to St Martin's-le-Grand. Catherine Street was at one time celebrated for the number of its newspaper offices; the "Court

Gazette" and "Court Journal", and "The Naval and Military Gazette" were published here. This street was also the birthplace of the first of the halfpenny papers, "The Echo", in 1868.

York Street connects Wellington Street with Drury Lane, and was named after James, Duke of York, afterwards James II. At one time this street only extended as far as Catherine Street, both Hatton and Strype describing it as "very short but well built and inhabited." It has been already stated that human remains are reported to have been unearthed here; and the very extensive vaults of some of the houses are said, according to Wheatley, to cover part of the burial ground of the ancient convent whence Covent Garden derived its name.

A tavern, known as the Fleece Inn, was situated here, "very unfortunate," says Aubrey, for homicides; three having happened within its walls in his time. Another tavern in this street, named the Turk's Head, enjoyed a more fortunate reputation.

About 1760–70 a theatrical club met here at a coffee-house named "Wright's." It was frequented by Foote, Holland, Porwell, and others. Former residents of York Street were Dr Donne's son in 1640; Mrs Pritchard, the actress, when she advertised her benefit at Drury Lane in "The Public Advertiser" of March 13, 1756; De Quincy at No. 4, where he wrote his "Confessions of an Opium Eater"; and Elliston, at No. 5, when lessee of Drury Lane Theatre. In York Street were situated the auction-rooms of Mr Samuel Baker, the originator of the celebrated firm of Messrs. Sotheby, Wilkinson & Hodge, whose present premises face the western frontage of Somerset House.

York Street leads into Tavistock Street, which, like other parts of the neighbourhood, has completely changed in appearance; the erection of the flower-market having swept away all the old houses which originally stood on the site, including Tavistock Row. This thoroughfare was celebrated as being the residence (No. 4) of the unfortunate Miss Ray, the beautiful mistress of Lord Sandwich, who was shot under the Piazza by a disappointed suitor, the Rev. James Hackman, in April 1779.

Hackman was once a lieutenant in the 68th Regiment of Foot, and, while on recruiting duty at Huntingdon, had been invited to Hitchinbrooke, the seat of Lord Sandwich, where he fell violently in love with his future victim. After repeated attempts to persuade her to become his wife, he determined, in a fit of maddening jealousy, to put an end to both their lives. He accordingly stationed himself under the Piazza, and, as she left Covent Garden Theatre, shot her first and himself afterwards. His wounds, however, did not prove fatal. He was tried for murder on April 17, and a few days later suffered the penalty of his crime at Tyburn. Miss Ray was once a milliner's apprentice at Clerkenwell. Her house was afterwards occupied by Macklin the elder, who died there in 1797.

> A Sandwich favourite was his fair,
> And her he clearly loved;
> By whom six children had, we hear;
> This story fatal proved.
> A clergyman, O wicked one!
> In Covent Garden shot her;
> No time to cry upon her God,
> It's hoped He's not forgot her.
>   (Grub Street ballad)

At No. 5 died William Vandervelde the younger in 1707, and in the same house died Thomas Major, the engraver, in 1799. The celebrated miniature-painter Zincke lived at No. 13; and in a garret in the same house lived Dr Wolcot (Peter Pindar), where he wrote against George III and the Royal Academy.

Close by are Burleigh and Exeter Streets, so named from being portions of the sites of Burleigh and Exeter Houses. In the latter street Dr Johnson took up his first abode in London at the house of a staymaker in 1737, where he lived on 4½d. a day.

Exeter House[1] was built on the site of another house constructed in the reign of Edward VI by Sir Thomas Palmer, who obtained the ground by composition. Here once stood a parsonage belonging to the Vicar of St Martin's-in-the-Fields. Sir Thomas Palmer was attainted and executed for high treason by Queen Mary, and the property then reverted to the Crown. Subsequently it was given by Queen Elizabeth to Sir William Cecil, Lord High Treasurer and afterwards the great Lord Burleigh, who completed the building with four square turrets. It was first named Cecil House, then Burleigh House, and afterwards Exeter House. Its Strand frontage extended as far west as Southampton Street. Its owner, Lord Burleigh, died at Theobalds in 1598, and his body lay in state here.

Here, too, lived Anthony Ashley Cooper, afterwards the first Earl of

Shaftesbury; and on February 26, 1671, his grandson, the author of the "Characteristics", was born in this mansion. Evelyn mentions in his Diary that he went to service on Christmas Day to Exeter Chapel in the Strand (the chapel belonging to Exeter House). "When the service was ended, and the Sacrament about to be administered, the chapel was surrounded by soldiers, and all the communicants and assembly surprised and kept prisoners. As we went up to receive the Sacrament, the miscreants held their muskets against us, as if they would have shot us at the altar, but yet suffering us to finish, the office of Communion, as perhaps not having instructions what to do in case they found us in that action." The diarist was kept prisoner in a room in Exeter House, and later in the day several officers came from Whitehall and examined him. "When I came before them," he writes, "they took my name and abode, examined me, why, contrary to an ordinance made, that none should any longer observe the superstitious time of the Nativity, I durst offend. Finding no colour to detain me," he adds, "they dismissed me with every pity of my ignorance."

At the south-west corner of Catherine Street formerly stood Wimbledon House, built by Sir William Cecil, third son of Thomas, Earl of Exeter, early in the seventeenth century. The former was created Viscount Wimbledon by Charles I. The mansion was burnt down in 1628, and its memory appears to have been quite forgotten in the vicinity. Part of its site, however, was afterwards used for the erection of D'Oyley's warehouse, which in its day resembled the modern stores. A full description of it appears in "The Gentleman's Magazine". The original founder, D'Oyley, was a French refugee, who is reputed to have escaped to this country on the revocation of the Edict of Nantes, and who went into business with some of his compatriots who had settled in Spitalfields, and who were engaged in the weaving trade, which industry was at that time being fostered by the English Government. D'Oyley appears to have made a success at once, and eventually the shop became the mart of taste, and his goods were considered as the leading mode. Steele, in "The Guardian", mentions his Doiley suit, and Dryden speaks of Doiley petticoats.

The old Gaiety Theatre and Restaurant were the successors of the Strand Music-hall, which occupied the site of a small arcade built by R. Smirke for the Marquis of Exeter, the owner of the property. This arcade ran from Catherine Street to Wellington Street, but did not prove a success like the Lowther Arcade, and was taken down in

1863. The old Gaiety was the home of burlesque, and opened with a performance of "Robert the Devil." It was pulled down in 1903, and a new Gaiety has been erected farther eastwards on the same side of the street. The old theatre was the scene of many a triumph of old favourites, who have, alas! gone to that bourne whence no traveller returns, such as Kate Vaughan, J.L. Toole, Nellie Farren, Edward Terry, and Katie Seymour.

The offices of "The Morning Post" were also rebuilt, when Aldwych was created for the Strand improvements. The first number of this paper appeared in 1772, just thirteen years before "The Times".

The site of the Lyceum Theatre was originally occupied by old Exeter House, and afterwards, according to Thornbury, by a building erected by the Society of Artists in 1765, "in anticipation of the royal establishment then in anticipation." Several exhibitions were held here, but the place soon became bankrupt, and, after under going considerable alterations, the rear portion was opened as a theatre, or place for variety entertainments. In 1802 Madame Tussaud's exhibition of waxworks was held there on her arrival in England from France. Fourteen years later the place was rebuilt, but was burnt down in 1830. It was rebuilt by Beazley somewhat farther west. In 1834 it was reopened with a performance of English opera, and it was not till another ten years had passed that a dramatic company performed there under the management of Mrs Keeley. The Beefsteak Club met here after quitting Covent Garden Theatre and the Bedford. The theatre was for many years the home of English drama under the direction of Sir Henry Irving. It has been rebuilt since his time; a new feature being the annual Christmas pantomime, and a great reduction in the price of seats; "popular prices" being the motto of the present Lyceum.

Exeter Change was situated in the Strand, on the west corner of Wellington Street, and extended as far as Burleigh Street, and was designed originally for commercial purposes. It was built by Dr Barbon, the speculator in houses in the reign of William and Mary. It is supposed that some of the materials of Exeter House were used in the construction of Exeter Change, including a pair of Corinthian columns. Exeter Street was built about the same time. It consisted of three spacious floors, and many varied exhibitions were held here, among which was a marvellous bed, which was at one time shown in the Adelphi. The building also appears to have been used as a mortuary, for in 1732 the body of Gay, the poet, lay here in state before its interment in Westminster Abbey. A few years later the body of Lord Baltimore rested there before being removed to Epsom. It was also at one time used as a storehouse for the printed volumes of the Rolls and Journals of the House of Lords. Some time afterwards Pidcock's Exhibition of Wild Beasts took up its abode in Exeter Change. This made the place an object of interest, especially to country-folk in London, whose admiration and curiosity were enhanced by the magnificent splendour of a mock Beefeater, who performed the duties of Commissionaire at the entrance. The menagerie was successively managed by three successive tenants, and it is said that the roars of the lions, distinctly heard in the Strand, frightened the horses very much. In 1826 a celebrated elephant, named Chunee, became unmanageable, and a squad of soldiers was told off to execute it. Exeter Change was taken down in 1828–9.

Opposite to the main entrance of the Lyceum in Wellington Street was a picturesque building famous as the first workshop of Charles Dickens, where "Household Words" was started. The building was graced by a large bay-window, almost immediately beneath which was the stage entrance to the old Gaiety Theatre.

A little higher up the street on the same side is the Victoria Club, chiefly resorted to by frequenters of the turf and other sportsmen.

Southampton Street has already been mentioned as being part of the site of Bedford House. This street was named after Lady Rachel, daughter of Thomas Wriothesley, Earl of Southampton, and wife of William, Lord Russell, the patriot. Here lived Mrs Oldfield, the actress; and at No. 27, David Garrick, previous to his removing to the Adelphi. In 1775 Garrick incurred the displeasure of the theatre-going public by including in his cast at Drury Lane a troup of French dancers. As war had already broken out between England and France, their appearance was hailed with great disapproval. He was unwise enough to allow them to appear on the following evening, when a riot ensued, and the mob, after destroying the scenery at the theatre, adjourned to his house and stoned the windows. The house is still known as Garrick House, and after being used as an hotel, has finally been let out as offices. The rooms are large and well lighted, although many have been made smaller to meet the requirements of business premises. In this street also was born Colley Cibber.

At the north end of Southampton Street stands the Covent Garden Hotel, once known as the Bedford Head Hotel, rebuilt in 1870. Horace

1. In the Saloon at Covent Garden. George & Robert Cruikshank for Pierce Egan's *Life in London*, 1821

2. Covent Garden Piazza. An engraved print by Edward Rooker from his *Six Views of London*, based on a drawing by Paul Sandby, 1768

3. Covent Garden Market

4. The north-west facade of the new Covent Garden Market, London, 1829. An illustration by T. Shepherd

5. The original entrance from the Piazza to the late Covent Garden Theatre. Destroyed by fire 20 September 1808

6. The Theatre Royal, Covent Garden, as altered previous to the opening on 15 September 1794. Destroyed by fire 20 September 1808

7. Inside the Covent Garden Theatre in 1847

8. The burning of the Theatre Royal, Covent Garden, in 1856

9. The exterior of the Theatre Royal, Covent Garden, in the nineteenth century

10. View of the east front of the new Theatre Royal, Covent Garden

11. North-west view of the Theatre Royal, Drury Lane,
from Great Russell Street

12. The interior of the old Theatre Royal,
Drury Lane, which burnt down in 1808

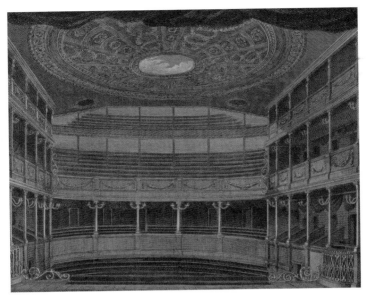

13. An internal view of the old Theatre Royal, Drury Lane,
as it appeared in 1792

14. The interior of the Theatre Royal, Drury Lane

Walpole, in his letters to Mann, November 20, 1741, says: "I believe I told you that Vernon's birthday passed off quietly, but it was not designed to be pacific; for at twelve at night eight gentlemen, dressed like sailors and masked, went round Covent Garden with a drum, beating up for a volunteer mob; but it did not take; and they retired to a great supper that was prepared for them at the Bedford Head, and ordered by Paul Whitehead, the author of 'Manners'."

Admiral Vernon, to whom Walpole refers, was at this period at the height of his popularity, on account of his successful attack upon Portobello in 1739, and the great gallantry he had shown on that occasion. His determined and violent opposition, as a member of Parliament, to the measures of the Government assisted in making him the idol of the mob, which he continued to be for many years (Cunningham).

Pope paid no compliment to this hotel when he wrote:

When sharp with hunger, scorn you to be fed,
Except on pea-chicks at the Bedford Head.

In 1711 Bohea tea, the cheapest of its kind, was sold at the "Barber's Pole" in Southampton Street at 26s. per lb. At No. 31 was the oldest chemist and druggist's shop in London, which was subsequently removed in 1863. The premises were the shop and laboratory of Ambrose Geoffrey Hanckwitz. Immediately after the discovery of phosphorus by Brandt the alchemist, Hanckwitz, under the directions of the celebrated Robert Boyle, succeeded in making an ounce of solid phosphorus. Such was the value of the newly discovered substance that it was sold for 50s. or 60s. the ounce. Hanckwitz's laboratory became a fashionable resort on certain occasions, when he performed experiments for the amusement of his friends (Timbs).

Here lived Ambrose Godfrey, of Godfrey & Cook. This gentleman was the inventor of a new process for extinguishing fire by "explosion and suffocation." The "machine" for this purpose was a kind of hollow wooden bomb filled with phosphorus and ignited by means of a fuse which in case of fire was to be lighted and thrown at the flames. The invention was extensively reported in the "Whitehall Evening Post" of 1724. The "machines," as the bombs were called, were manufactured by a joiner named Briggs in Salisbury Street, Strand. The largest size cost 25s., the second size 21s., and the smallest 18s. Those used for chimney fires were called "chimney shells" and were sold at 10s. 6d. and 7s. 6d.

Maiden Lane is a narrow street connecting Southampton Street with Bedford Street. In the parish books of St Paul's, Covent Garden, Maiden Lane is described as being "behind the Bull Inn."

In this street resided Andrew Marvell, the poet and patriot, when he was visited by Lord Danby with a message from the King offering him favours, which he refused to accept. Marvell first became acquainted with the Commonwealth through his appointment as tutor to the daughter of Lord Fairfax. He was afterwards recommended by Milton, who had become totally blind, for the post of his Assistant Secretary for Foreign Affairs. Marvell may be described as the poet of Cromwell and the Protectorate. The story of the visit of Lord Dandy to him, and the offer from the King which the poet refused, first appeared in Cook's Life of Marvell in 1726. According to this authority, when the poet had been entertained one night by the King, who had often been delighted in his company, his Majesty the next day sent Danby to discover his lodging. Danby found Marvell writing "up two pairs of stairs in a little court in the Strand," and announced that he came with a message from his Majesty, which was to know what he could do to serve him Marvell answered "that it was not in his Majesty's power to serve him." Danby then definitely offered him a place at Court, which was refused with the retort "that he could not accept with honour, for he must be either ungrateful to the King in voting against him, or false to his country in giving in to the measures of the Court; therefore, the only favour he begged of his Majesty was that he would esteem him as dutiful a subject as any he had, and more in his proper interests in refusing his offers than if he had embraced them." Finding farther persuasion useless, Danby then told him that the King had ordered a thousand pounds for him, which he hoped he would receive till he could think what further he could ask of his Majesty. This last offer was refused as steadfastly as the first, although, as soon as the Treasurer had departed, "he was forced to send to a friend to borrow a guinea."

Here lived Archbishop Sancroft, when Dean both of York and St Paul's in 1663.

At a hairdresser's shop named the "White Peruke," Voltaire resided when he visited this country after his liberation from the Bastille. He lived here for some years, and obtained many subscriptions towards his "Henriade," besides making the acquaintance of his literary contemporaries, Pope, Young, Congreve, and others. During his stay in London Voltaire perfected himself in the language to such an extent that he was able to read and write it like a native. This knowledge once carried him safely through an uncomfortable situation. While out walking he was ridiculed for a Frenchman, but, getting into a doorway, he so harangued his tormentors in English in praise of British liberty, and the British nation generally, that the mob hailed him as a jolly good fellow, and carried him shoulder-high to his lodging in Maiden Lane.

Here also was born J.M.W. Turner, the celebrated painter, who resided here till 1800, when he was elected Associate of the Royal Academy. His father was a hairdresser, and Turner, when a boy, coloured prints for Mr J.R. Smith, a mezzotint engraver, who lived in the same street. During the period of his stay in Maiden Lane he exhibited fifty-nine pictures at the Academy (Timbs).

The far-famed Cider Cellars were situated in this street, the haunt of Professor Porson. This establishment was a kind of old-fashioned tavern, celebrated for devilled kidneys and Welsh rarebits, which were consumed to the accompaniment of a rousing chorus. The place has been described by Charles Lamb in "The London Magazine". Opposite resided Proctor, the sculptor, in very reduced circumstances. Richard Porson (1759–1808) was born near North Walsham in Norfolk, where his father, Huggin Porson, a worsted weaver, was parish clerk. In his early days he showed remarkable powers of memory, which attracted the attention of the vicar of the parish. Through his instrumentality Porson was sent to be examined at Cambridge, where he satisfied his examiners so amply that his influential friends sent him to pursue his studies at Eton, where he remained four years. He then entered Trinity College, Cambridge, in 1778, and was admitted to a professorship in 1792. He afterwards resided in London, and had lodgings in the Temple. He died September 25, 1808, and was buried in the chapel of Trinity College. Porson was an exceedingly proud man, and declined most invitations from the fashionable world, saying that "they only wanted to see me out of curiosity, and, when that was satisfied, they would like to kick me down the stairs." It was on this account that he refused to dine at Holland House to meet Fox, who had expressed a wish to make the acquaintance of the famous Greek scholar.

Many quaint stories are told of this eccentric but homely genius, of which the following is a good example. Porson was once travelling in a stage-coach, when one of the passengers, in the course of conversation, quoted some Greek verses, which he ascribed to Euripides as their writer. Porson gravely extracted a volume from his coat-tail pocket and said, "This, Sir, is a copy of Euripides; the verses are not there to my knowledge, but perhaps you can show them to me." The gentleman, somewhat confused, corrected himself, and said that he meant Sophocles. Applying his hand to another pocket, Porson produced a Sophocles, with the same invitation. "Well, well," said the perturbed stranger, "perhaps after all it was Æschylus." But upon seeing Porson in the act of drawing forth a third volume, he jumped up in extreme agitation, and called out to the driver, "Coachman, stop the coach, and let me out. This is either Porson or the Devil!"

On the south side of the street was the Maiden Lane Synagogue, situated on the first floor of No. 21, to gain access to which it was necessary to mount a flight of stairs. At one time it boasted an important congregation, most of the Jewish salesmen in the market being members; but, owing to the migration of its supporters from the district, it has recently amalgamated with the new West End Synagogue, St Alban's Place, in the Haymarket. The place is now used as a miniature theatre for rehearsals, and is fitted up with every convenience for the purpose. Next door is the stage entrance to the Adelphi Theatre, and it was here that poor William Terriss was murdered some years ago by a lunatic who was ordered to be detained in custody during her late Majesty's pleasure. William Terriss will be remembered as being the father of the charming Miss Ellaline Terriss, the wife of Mr Seymour Hicks.

Opposite is "Rule's," an establishment renowned for its oysters and other shell-fish. Maiden Lane is now entirely occupied by theatrical agencies.

Henrietta Street, which runs parallel with Maiden Lane, was built in 1637, and named after Henrietta Maria, the wife of Charles I. When first erected it was a most fashionable street. Among the names of its early inhabitants I find those of Strafford, Lord-Lieutenant of Ireland, who resided in a house on the south side in 1640, Sir Lewis Dives in 1637, Samuel Cooper the miniature-painter in 1645, Kitty Clive the actress, McArdell the engraver, and Sir Robert Strange at the sign of the "Golden Head," of whom the latter is buried in St Paul Church.

In 1774 Paul Whitehead, the poet, and author of "Manners", died in this street. Horace Walpole describes him as "an infamous, but not despicable poet." Mr Peter Cunningham is more severe in his criticism, and describes him as a most profligate individual; "the boon companion of Sir Francis Dashwood, Churchill, Wilkes, and others; being, like them, a member of the Hell-fire Club, which held its orgies at Medmenham Abbey in Buckinghamshire." The estimation in which he was held even by his friends may be judged by the lines in which Churchill has "damned him to everlasting fame":

> May I (can worse disgrace on manhood fall?)
> Be born a Whitehead, and baptized a Paul.

At Rawthmell's coffee-house the Society of Arts was established in 1754; and at the Castle Tavern, also situated in this street, Sheridan fought and disarmed Mathews, his rival for the affections of Miss Linley (Cunningham).

At No. 23 was "Offley's," a celebrated eating-house celebrated for its chops. The proprietor was originally at "Bellamy's," close by the House of Commons, and evidently enjoyed considerable prosperity. "Offley's" chops were considerably larger than Bellamy's, because we read that honourable members thought nothing of eating a dozen at one sitting at the latter establishment. "Offley's" was much frequented for supper, and in the great room one evening each week was singing, where Francis Carew sang Moore's melodies, then in the height of their fame (Macmichael's "Charing Cross"). A surgical instrument maker from the Strand was an habitué. This gentleman bought the iron off the piles of old London Bridge, where it had been for several hundred years soaking in the Thames, and from it made some of the finest surgical instruments ever known (Timbs, "Walks and Talks London").

The north side of Henrietta Street has been entirely rebuilt, the London County and Westminster Bank occupying fine premises there; while a little lower down on the same side is St Peter's Hospital for the treatment of the bladder, kidney, and venereal disorders; on the south side is situated St Paul's Rectory, and the remainder of the houses are, almost without exception, occupied by publishers.

1. See Appendix.

XI

*Bedford and King Streets—Half Moon Street—
Celebrated residents—Clay's papier-mâché trays—Civil
Service Stores—The Garrick Club—Thackeray and
Dickens and other members—Mahogany wood in King
Street—The Indian chiefs—The Essex Serpent—Samuel
Taylor Coleridge—Mr J.C. Stevens' auction-rooms—
New Street—Dr Johnson at the "Pine-apple"—
Bedfordbury—Sir Francis Kynaston and the Museum
Minerva—Garrick Street and Rose Street—Butler—
Chandos Street and its balconies—Sally Salisbury*

Bedford Street, as were several of its neighbours after the Great Fire, was chiefly inhabited by prosperous and well-to-do merchants. Strype writes: "A handsome broad street with very good houses, which, since the Fire of London, are generally taken up by eminent tradesmen, as mercers, lacemen, drapers, and men of other trades, as are King Street and Henrietta Street. But the west side of this street is the best." It lies between King Street and Maiden Lane, and is connected with the Strand by Half Moon Street, so named after a tavern of this name which stood there, and is mentioned by Ned Ward in his "London Spy".

Here lived Remigius van Limput, the painter, who purchased the portrait of Charles I on horseback by Van Dyck at the sale of that unfortunate monarch's effects; but at the Restoration he was forced to give up his treasure. Whether he was paid for it or not, is not known; but the picture is now at Windsor Castle.

In 1635 Chief Justice Richardson was living in a house on the west side; Sir Francis Kynaston in 1637; and De Grammont's Earl of Chesterfield in 1656. Another resident was Thomas Sheridan, the father of Richard Brinsley Sheridan. From this house was noticed the peculiar habit of Dr Johnson (related by Mr Whyte in his "Miscellanea Nova") of making, in his passage to and fro, a rule of touching each of the posts which at that period were placed at regular intervals along the curb to prevent passing vehicles from encroaching on the footpath. Quin, the actor, lived here from 1749 to 1752.

In a house in the south-east corner of this street lived Clay, who made a fortune in 1760 by applying the use of papier-mâché to tea-trays. Clay was a pupil of Baskerville of Birmingham. Many of his trays were painted by some of the earliest members of the Royal Academy, amongst whom was Wheatley. At the corner of Bedford and Chandos Streets lived Humphrey Wanley, the antiquary, in 1718. The house was known as the Riding-hood Shop. The opposite corner is now occupied by the West-end branch of the Civil Service Stores.

King Street was named after Charles I, and was built in 1637. At No. 35 the Garrick Club was first established in 1834, where it flourished for thirty years before moving to its present home in Garrick Street. The building is now occupied by the Capital and Counties Bank and Messrs. Hicks, Arnold & Mozeley, solicitors. This house was originally the home of William Lewis, the comedian, and the premises were afterwards occupied by an hotel known as Probatt's. King Street has always been connected with Garrick, who resided in it for some time at the house of a Mr West, a cabinet-maker.

The Club was founded by Mr Frank Mills in 1831, whose object is thus stated: "To found a Society in which actors and men of education and refinement might meet on equal terms"—a significant statement, indicating the social position of the actor of that period, who was only then emerging from his previous condition of "rogue and vagabond." The formation of the Garrick stands at the parting of the ways, where the old rough-and-ready tavern life, into which the coffee-houses had degenerated, was passing into a more staid and correct meeting-place for social intercourse. Thackeray joined the Club in 1833, and may be regarded as the leading light of the institution. Dickens joined four years later, but after twice resigning his membership, he finally quitted the Club in 1865.

The opening of the Club was celebrated by a sumptuous dinner in 1832, which was presided over by the Duke of Sussex, its official patron. In the list of famous members figure the names of Macready, Charles Mathews, Planché, the Duke of Sussex, Lord Sydney, Robert Walpole, Charles Young, Fred Yates, jun., Theodore Hook of immortal fame, the Marquis of Anglesea, Earl of Belfast, Earl of Fife, Duke of Devonshire, the Marquis of Clanricarde, the Rev. R.H. Barham ("Thomas Ingoldsby"), and Charles Kemble. The present building in Garrick Street was constructed by Mr Marrable, and opened in 1862 (see Garrick Street).

Of the Rev. R.H. Barham, who in his "Ingoldsby Legends" opened out a totally fresh and unhackneyed style of humorous verse, the following story is told. One of his fellow-clerics, whose sense of humour, if it ever existed, was overlaid by a superincumbent mass of dulness and piety, complained to his (and Barham's) Bishop that Barham had written a book of very profane verse. The Bishop asked Barham for an explanation. Barham sent him his book. Whether the Bishop's sense of humour overmastered his sense of religious propriety or not is unknown, but it is certain that Barham never received any episcopal reproof.

The Club possesses a fine collection of portraits of theatrical celebrities of the past, and was first started by Charles Mathews the elder. Mathews was a good-natured individual, but, like most of his kidney, entirely devoid of business methods, and incapable of appreciating the value of money. Although he commanded big salaries, he was never in affluent circumstances. He betted and gambled; was imposed upon by his friends and fleeced by strangers. He had a penchant for pictures; and the dealers, knowing their customer, made him pay dearly for his hobby. In later days, when in need of ready money, he sold many of his more valuable specimens, and had copies made of them, which suited his purpose just as well. The collection reached large dimensions, and he was persuaded to exhibit it to the public, for which purpose he rented a large room in a house in Oxford Street. Alas! his expectations of a financial success were sadly shattered. The exhibition resulted in a net loss of £150. His friends advised him to sell, but he could not be induced to part with his cherished pictures.

A proposal that the collection should be purchased by the Club somewhat modified his unwillingness to resign his hold upon them, but the sum offered was so small that the negotiations were dropped.

The collection numbered in all 415 canvases; not all these, however, were separate portraits, there being many studies of the same individual. The gems of the collection are those of Badderley, Bannister, and Garrick. There are also portraits of Edmund Kean, John Kemble, Charles Kemble, Charles Mathews, Quin, Mrs Woffington, and many others. A selection of the best examples came eventually into the possession of Mr R. Durrant, who presented it to the Club in 1852, when it still occupied its old premises.

There was also a large assortment of Garrick relics, amongst which is a chair made out of the stage of old Drury Lane Theatre. There is also his silver ticket of admission to the Haymarket Theatre, his dress sword and shoe buckles, and the medal worn by him when steward of the Stratford Commemoration in 1769, and also two chairs from his villa at Hampton. There is also the ivory pass which belonged to Mrs Garrick, entitling her to pass through the gates of the Park. The history of this celebrated Club has been fully written by Mr Percy Fitzgerald, from whose work much of this information has been derived.

In King Street mahogany first came into vogue. When Dr Gibbons was building his house in this street, his brother, a West India merchant, sent over some of the wood as ballast, thinking it might prove of some use to his brother. This species of wood was unknown at the time in this country, and when the carpenters set to work on it, they found it too hard for their tools. The doctor, some time after, ordered a box to be made from it. When this had been accomplished with the aid of specially made tools, the result was much admired. A bureau was then made, and the fine colour and polish were so pleasing that the worthy doctor invited his friends to come and inspect it. Amongst the latter was the Duchess of Buckingham, through whose patronage the wood came into general use. Many of the front doors of the King Street houses were long celebrated for being made of solid mahogany. ("History of Charing Cross" by Macmichael).

In this street resided the North American Indian chiefs who visited England in the reign of Queen Anne in order to obtain the assistance they requested against the French in Canada. They remained here for about a fortnight, were lavishly entertained, and taken to see the sights of the metropolis.

"The Tatler" says that they were "clothed and entertained at the public expense, while continuing in London, in a handsome apartment." There is no doubt that their landlord was an upholsterer in Covent Garden. On April 18, 1710, the visitors were conveyed in two of the royal carriages to St James's by Sir Charles Cotterell, Master of the Ceremonies, and introduced by the Earl of Shaftesbury, the Lord Chamberlain. Their speech, which was translated by a Major Pidgeon, who had accompanied them from America, was to the effect that "they had, with one consent, hung up the kettle and taken up the hatchet, in token of their great queen and her children, and had been, on the other side of the great water, a strong wall of security to their great queen's children, even to the loss of their best men." They added that "they had always considered the French as men of falsehood, and rejoiced in the prospect of the reduction of Canada; after which they should have free hunting and a great trade with their great queen's children; and as a token of the sincerity of the six nations, in the name of all, they presented their great queen with the belts of the wampum" (Leigh Hunt's "The Town").

On the south side of King Street a public-house rejoicing in the curious name of the "Essex Serpent," a name which is ascribed by certain writers to a legendary and formidable dragon supposed to haunt a portion of Essex at the time when King Street was built. In a house situated on the site of the present Westminster Fire Office lived Lenthal, Speaker of the House of Commmons in the time of the Commonwealth. Here lived Quin, the actor, and also Nicholas Rowe, editor of Shakespeare and author of "Jane Shore". Another poet lived in this street, viz. Samuel Taylor Coleridge, from 1799 to 1802, when earning a precarious livelihood as an obscure writer on political subjects to "The Morning Post".

King Street was long renowned for its numerous print-shops, but only one or two remain to-day. A few doors westwards from the National Sporting Club are the auction-rooms of Mr J.C. Stevens, where sales are held weekly of all kinds of miscellaneous property and also bulbs and plants in their proper season. This firm was established in 1776. The premises occupied by Mr Stevens were first tenanted by the celebrated auctioneer, Mr Paterson, who was the first of his profession to offer books singly, in lots. He was an exceedingly well read man and was commonly supposed to have read every book in the English language that he offered for sale. He eventually became librarian to the Marquis of Lansdowne. The premises were then taken by Messrs. King, Collins & Chapman, who also sold books and prints. Mr. J.T. Smith's "Nollekens and his Times" mentions the fact that here Charles Dibden commenced his "London Amusement", and here his popular song "Poor Jack" was so often encored (Macmichael's "Charing Cross"). The auction-rooms of Messrs. King & Locke, chiefly for books, were also situated in this street.

In this street are also the spacious premises of Messrs. Verity & Co., the electrical engineers. On the south side is also Messrs. Barr & Sons, the seed experts and nurserymen. Messrs. Geo. Monro, Ltd., are established in a handsome building adjoining the National Sporting Club, and also occupy the shop on the south-east corner of the street.

King Street leads westwards into a very narrow thoroughfare, named New Street, which runs as far as St Martin's Lane nearly opposite the New Theatre. Even this narrow little street was fashionably inhabited in the reign of Charles II. The Countess of Chesterfield, of whom the great painter Van Dyck was enamoured, lived in a house on the south side in 1660. Flaxman, the sculptor, also lived here in 1771–2.

It was at a tavern named the "Pine-apple" that Dr Johnson used to dine when he first came to London. "I dined," said he, "very well for eightpence, with very good company, at the Pine Apple in New Street. Several of them had travelled. They expected to meet every day, but did not know one another's names. It used to cost the others a shilling, for they drank wine; but I had a cut of meat for sixpence, and bread for a penny, and gave the waiter a penny; so that I was quite well served, aye! better than the rest, for they gave the waiter nothing."

Connecting New Street and Chandos[1] Street is Bedfordbury, a small, narrow street, of late greatly improved by the addition of the rear portion of the Coliseum; for which purpose a large number of miserable houses and courts were pulled down. Mr Robert Allbutt, in his "Rambles in Dickens' Land", says that this district was the dreadful slum depicted by Dickens in "Bleak House" as Tom's All-alone. Mr Cunningham, in his invaluable handbook, records the fact that Sir Francis Kynaston, scholar and poet, lived here about 1638–40, "on the east side of the street towards Berrie." It was at the house of this gentleman in the "Garden" that an Academy, called the Museum Minerva, was established in the reign of Charles I. for the instruction and education of the young members of the nobility and gentry in the arts and foreign languages, etc. Sir Francis was president of the institution, and, on the outbreak of the Plague, petitioned the King for permission to remove to Chelsea College; but, on account of the opposition manifested by the authorities of the latter establishment, probably from a reasonable fear of contagion, Sir Francis was compelled to seek other quarters, in the same neighbourhood, however, as the College.

Garrick Street was constructed for the purpose of providing a means of extra access to the market from the west end, for which purpose it was found necessary to cut through a large number of houses and Rose Street, and was named after the Garrick Club, established here after its removal from King Street. The former was a narrow street which ran in a zigzag fashion from Long Acre to the corner of New Street. The new road was commenced in 1855 and completed about 1861, and the cost of the undertaking amounted to £34,000, towards which the Duke of Bedford contributed £1,500.

Rose Street[2] will be remembered as the scene of the assault on the poet Dryden, narrated in a previous chapter. Here also died Butler, the author of "Hudibras", who is buried in St Paul's Church. In this street also lived Mr Edmund Curll, bookseller, and publisher of Pope's Literary Correspondence.

In Rose Street, immediately behind the premises of Messrs. Debenham, Storr & Sons at the corner of Garrick and King Streets, is a public-house of some antiquity named the "Lamb and Flag." These are the armorial bearings of the Middle Temple, but I am unable to account for any connection with this part, unless, as Mr Macmichael suggests in his "History of Charing Cross", some former servant of the Templars set up the sign.

Chandos Street was named after William Brydges, Lord Chandos, grandfather of the "magnificent Duke." Here Duval, the highwayman, was captured at a tavern known as the "Hole in the Wall."

In this street was one of the first houses that boasted a balcony, which, when first erected, caused a great deal of curiosity. Balconies were first introduced into London in the neighbourhood of Covent Garden, and probably the one in Chandos Street was amongst the first examples. In a house of ill-fame in this street the Hon. John Finch was stabbed by a certain lady named Sally Salisbury, who was thus styled on account of a fancied resemblance to the Countess of that name. She died in Newgate whilst undergoing her sentence for this deed of violence. Besides leaving behind her a portrait by Kneller, she is described by Mr Caulfield in his "Memoirs of Remarkable Persons" as having "the character of the most notorious woman that ever infested the Hundreds of Old Drury, or Covent Garden either."

1. See Appendix.
2. See Appendix.

XII

Long Acre—Original name—Abode of the coach-makers—The Duke's Bagnio: a description—The ale-houses—Prior and Chloë—The Water-poet—Covent Garden quacks—Partridge and Bickerstaff—James Street: celebrated residents—St Martin's Hall—Charles Dickens—The Sun public-house and Ben Jonson

At the time when the Convent Garden, as it was then called, was surrounded by a brick wall, the thoroughfare that is to-day known as Long Acre was a straggling footpath leading from St Martin's Lane to Drury Lane. At that period there were no houses between Covent Garden and the tiny hamlet of St Giles-in-the-Fields. Long Acre is of great antiquity. The earliest mention I have been able to trace is in 1556, when it was mentioned by Machyn in his Diary on December 6th of that year: "The murder of one Richard Eggylston in the Long Acurs, the bak syd of Charinge-Crosse."

It was also known as the Elms, on account of some fine elm trees which stood there and whose grateful shade was much appreciated by the worthy citizens, who much frequented it in the summer months. When the property was laid out, after coming into the hands of the Bedford family, it received its present name from the fact that its reputed area was just one acre.

In 1656 Howell described it as a "spacious fair street." From its earliest days it has been the home of the carriage builder, many of the best-known firms having their premises here. Even before the street was built a blacksmith's forge was in existence at the Holborn end of Drury Lane. Perhaps the earliest of the coach-builders was one

John Sanders, of Long Acre, coachmaker, who was fined the sum of £12 in 1695 for not serving the office of overseer (St Martin's Parish Accounts).

Thomas Stothard, the painter, was the son of a coachmaker residing in this street.

Most of the streets leading out of Long Acre are exceedingly narrow, and are known as courts. Banbury Court was named after Banbury House, which stood on its site, and was inhabited by the Earl of Peterborough in 1673. There was also a Lumley Court, named after Lady Lumley, who resided there in 1660.

Salisbury Court, on the south side of the street, adjoined a celebrated establishment known as the Duke's Bagnio, or Sweating House, of which a full description appears in Malcolm's "Londinium Redivivum", vol. iv. The manager was Sir W. Jennings, who resided next door, and who, in reward for his services to the throne, obtained from the King a patent for the making of all the public bagnios and baths in the metropolis. The place appears to have been very well conducted for a number of years, but subsequently followed the downward path of other similar places. The bath was for the use of both sexes on different days. On the accession of the Duke of York to the throne as James II the baths assumed a regal title, having been originally named after the Duke. In 1686 a handbill was published by the then proprietor, Mr Leonard Cundit, who advertised the bath under the title of the King's Bagnio.

There was also a Spa, or well of medicinal waters, described as "artificially made, by mineral principles, conveyed into the earth by appropriate vessels, there springing up in a sufficient quantity to supply all persons that shall have occasion to drink them. The colour is clear and transparent, the taste sweet and somewhat styptic. The waters turn purple if mixed with galls, and are reduced to transparency by a few drops of spirit of vitriol: oyl of tartar per deliquium will curdle and turn them white, and spirit of vitriol will restore them to their former pellucid colour."

The well was covered over with stone, and ornamented with a statue "with much carved work about it." The well was close to the wall of the bath-house in the yard, and was encompassed on that side with tall palisadoes, in which there was a door made for the person who drew the water to pass to the well, and a window, out of which the water was handed to those who required it. There was also a waiting-room for the drinkers to sit in and sip the mixture, which, according to the nature of all such beverages, could not have been of too pleasurable a nature; and probably suggested, as Sam Weller said of the waters at Bath, a taste of flat-iron.

In 1694 the bath was greatly altered and improved in the system of heating, which at the Hummums could not have been properly regulated, the fires being placed immediately under the hot-rooms, while here they were situated farther off. The price of admission for a single person was 5s., but if two came together reduction of 1s. each was made on the charge.

Adjoining the Bagnio was a coffee-house named the Duke's Bagnio Coffee-house, at the side of which was the principal entrance to the baths.

When George I came to the throne, and party feeling ran high between Whigs and Tories, Long Acre became celebrated for its mug-houses or ale-houses, where beer-drinking clubs were held, and where politics were "sung or said." Defoe, in his "Journey through England", gives an excellent description of these places, for which Cheapside was also renowned, but the chief centre appears to have been Long Acre:—

"But the most diverting and amusing of all is the Mug-house Club in Long Acre; where every Wednesday and Saturday a mixture of Gentlemen, Lawyers, and Tradesmen meet in a great Room, and are seldom under a hundred. They have a grave old Gentleman, in his own grey hairs, now within a few months of 90 years old, who is their President, and sits in an arm'd chair some steps higher than the rest of the Company, to keep the whole Room in order. A harp plays all the time at the other end of the Room; and every now and then one or other of the company rises and entertains the rest with a song, and (by the by) some are good masters. Here is nothing drank but ale, and every gentleman hath his separate Mug, which he chalks on the Table where he sits, a it is brought in; and every one retires when he pleases, as from a Coffee-house. The room is always so diverted with Songs and drinking from one Table to another to one another's Healths, that there is no room for Politicks, or anything that can sow'r conversation. One must be there by seven to get room, and after ten the Company are for the most part gone. This is a Winter's Amusement, that is agreeable enough to a Stranger for once or twice, and he is well diverted with the different Humours, when the Mugs overflow. ...

"On King George's Accession to the Throne, the Tories had so much the better of the Friends to the Protestant Succession, that they gained the Mobs on all Publick Days to their side. This induced a Sett of Gentlemen to establish Mug-houses in all the corners of this great city, for well-affected Tradesmen to meet and keep up the Spirit of Loyalty to the Protestant Succession, and to be ready upon all Tumults to join their Forces for the Suppression of the Tory mobs. Many an encounter they had, and many were the riots, till at last the Parliament was obliged by an Act to put an end to this City strife, which had this good effect, that upon pulling down of the Mug-house in Salisbury Court, for which some boys were hanged on this Act, the City has not been troubled with them since."

In this street was a shoemaker's shop with two windows; in one were placed pairs of boots and shoes, and in the other a picture by Richard Wilson, the landscape painter; and it is more than probable that many a picture that was then picked up for a few pounds has since realised as many hundreds.

In Long Acre resided "Chloë," the object of Prior's affection, whom he compares in his verses to Venus and Diana. Some say she was the wife of a cobbler, others of a soldier. Whoever she was, she does not appear to have met with the approbation of the poet's friends. Pope says: "Everybody knows what a wretch she was"; and, "Prior was not a right good man. He used to bury himself for whole days and nights together with a poor mean creature, and often drank hard."

Pope's friend, Richardson, says that Prior, after having spent the evening in the company of Swift, Bolingbroke, Pope, and Oxford, would go and smoke a pipe and drink a bottle of ale with a common soldier and his wife in Long Acre, before going to bed (Leigh Hunt, "The Town").

One of the first taverns in this street was situated in Phœnix Alley, and was kept by John Taylor, a contemporary of Shakespeare, who, though originally a Thames waterman, aspired to the dignity of a poet. At the death of Charles I he called his house "The Mourning Crown," but during the Commonwealth he adorned his signboard with his own portrait, together with the following motto:

> There's many a head stands for a sign;
> Then, gentle reader, why not mine?

Although Taylor regarded coaches as his natural enemy, he continued to reside amongst them, and died in 1653.

Mr Timbs mentions that among the nostrums sold in Long Acre were Dr Gardner's worm-destroying medicines, and Burchell's anodyne necklaces, strongly recommended for teeth-cutting by Dr Turner, the inventor, and by Dr Chamberlain, who is said to have possessed the secret.

The neighbourhood of Covent Garden was the happy hunting-ground for the quacks and fortune-tellers. When the Plague broke out, many were the wonderful concoctions sold to a credulous and panic-stricken populace under the title of "Cure." Of the quacks who dealt in these cures, perhaps the best known was Partridge, who was also an almanac maker. This individual, who resided at different date in both Henrietta Street and James Street, was the butt of the wits of the period. He foretold the death of the King of France, which prophecy was turned to ridicule by Swift in the following manner. Writing under the name of Bickerstaff, Swift foretold the death of Partridge at a certain date. When the appointed period duly arrived, Swift insisted that Partridge was, *ipso facto*, dead. Partridge gravely informed the public that he was, on the contrary, very much alive. Bickerstaff, however, still insisted on the correctness of his own view, to the amusement of the whole town and to the acute distress of the putative corpse. Partridge repeatedly advertised the fact of his continued existence, but in the end was compelled to give up making almanacs, the prognostications of a dead man not being a marketable commodity.

In his almanac for 1707 he writes: "Whereas it has been industriously given out by Bickerstaff and others, to prevent the sale of this year's almanac, that John Partridge is dead, this may inform all his loving countrymen that, blessed be God, he is still living in health, and they are knaves who reported otherwise."

Stukeley claimed to have discovered a "tumulus" or burial place of ancient Britons in Long Acre, but the evidence is not at all trustworthy. A burial ground belonging to the Quakers was at one time situated near Salisbury Court, but it passed out of their hands in 1757 and the site was used for building purposes ("London Burial Grounds", by Mrs B. Holmes).

Before pursuing our investigations farther along Long Acre we must not forget James Street, which connects Long Acre with the north side of the market proper. This street was built about 1637, and named after James, Duke of York, afterwards James II, as was also York Street. Here lived Sir Henry Herbert, brother of Lord Herbert of Cherbury, and of Sir George Herbert, once Master of the Revels. His house was on the west side, almost at the corner of Hart Street. No. 77 was the residence of another of the artistic fraternity, to wit, Charles Grignon, the engravor, who died in 1810.

In James Street resided a mysterious lady, who arrived from Mansfield in 1714 in a coach drawn by six horses. She died in 1720, and was supposed to have been a member of an old Catholic family who had been in her early days consigned to a convent, whence she had been liberated by a relative. She was buried in the neighbouring St Paul's churchyard.

The *dernier cri* in modernism is the Covent Garden Station of the Piccadilly and Brompton Railway, at the corner of James Street and Long Acre.

On the north side of the latter thoroughfare still stand the huge premises lately vacated by the celebrated firm of brewers, Messrs. Watney, Coombe & Reid. This extensive block of buildings is now being rapidly converted into fruit warehouses.

Farther along the street, on the same side, but at the corner of Endell Street, stands a large building lately occupied by Kestertons, the carriage builders. It has now become tenanted by a large firm of publishers and printers. Adjoining it is an edifice which once boasted a considerable reputation as a place of amusement. It was originally known as St Martin's Hall, built in 1847 by William Cubitt. It was opened three years later as a music-hall, in which many concerts and oratorios of a high class were given. Here Charles Dickens gave his first series of sixteen readings in London, under the management of Arthur Smith, in 1858. The hall was also utilised for political meetings. Like other places of amusement, it suffered the usual fate of being burnt down, which calamity occurred in 1860, the fire originating next door, at Kestertons'. It was rebuilt, and again opened as a concert-hall, but did not long subserve this purpose. After having been altered and rebuilt, it was opened as a theatre, under the name of the Queen's, which title had just been discarded by the old theatre in Windmill Street, Tottenham Court Road, rechristened the Prince of Wales's. Many artists of distinction appeared here, such as J.L. Toole, Phelps, and Mr and Mrs Rousby.

The Queen's (new) Theatre was closed in 1875, and the building was converted into a "stores." It is now a seed warehouse.

Opposite, at the corner of Bow Street, stands the warehouse of Messrs. Merryweather, fire-engine makers. Farther down, on the same side as the latter establishment, are the large printing-offices of "The Gentlewoman" and "John Bull."

In Long Acre was a tavern of some renown called the Sun, and frequented by Ben Jonson. Whether the present public-house of this name in Broad Court is the same is not certainly known. The story goes that Ben Jonson one day went to another of his city haunts for a drink (poets have always been thirsty souls, from Anacreon and Horace downwards), to wit, the Half Moon in Aldersgate Street, but, finding it closed, he walked on as far as the Sun in Long Acre, where he indited the following quatrain:

> Since the Half Moon is so unkind
> To make me go about,
> The Sun my money now shall have,
> The Moon shall go without."

Endell Street was formerly divided, and called Old and New Belton Streets.[1] Its chief building is the Lying-in Hospital, the oldest institution of its kind in London. It formerly occupied premises in Brownlow Street, since renamed Betterton Street. This street was named after Sir John Brownlow, whose house and gardens stood on the spot. He resided here between 1676 and 1682, and it is thought that the Charity occupied part of the original mansion after it was vacated. Michael Mohun, the actor, died in Brownlow Street in 1684.

At the rear of No. 25, Endell Street, are to be found the reputed remains of an old bath, which was fed by a stream of clear water, boasting certain medicinal qualities, useful in curing gout and rheumatism. It was known as Queen Anne's Bath, but whether it was ever patronised by her Majesty is a matter of conjecture; and since we know that "Queen Anne is dead," she cannot be cross-examined in verification (or the reverse) of the rumour.

The shop is now occupied by a firm of ironmongers, and the bath, or rather what remains of it, is now a lumber-room.

The celebrated Lewkner's Lane, mentioned previously, is now named Macklin Street. It was, from its earliest days, a street of evil repute, and later it became quite renowned for its vicious inhabitants. Jonathan Wild, the thief-taker, ran a house of ill-repute here. Mr Cunningham assigns to it the same unsavoury reputation as late as 1850.

1. See Appendix.

XIII

Covent Garden as we know it to-day

After this review of the immediate neighbourhood of Covent Garden there yet remains for our investigation the market proper. From the preceding chapters we have seen how the market became established by the regular gathering of a few itinerant vendors of fruit and vegetables from the surrounding villages. Its growth in commercial importance has gradually but surely increased, in spite of the competition of other markets which have been established at different periods in various parts of the metropolis. I have already referred to Farringdon Market, which at one time was a serious rival to Covent Garden and might even have eventually eclipsed it in importance had it not been for the erection of Waterloo Bridge, which gave a long-desired access to the western market and which was immediately taken advantage of by the Surrey and Kentish growers.

Hungerford Market was established in 1679 on the site of Hungerford House, Charing Cross. The first market-building was designed by Sir Christopher Wren, the architect of St Paul's Cathedral. Sir Edward Hungerford, a famous spendthrift, after having exhausted the family fortune, thought to again enrich himself by the formation of a market, and, after obtaining the King's permission, erected stalls and buildings on the site of the family residence, Hungerford House, which had been destroyed by fire on April 25, 1669. Like its neighbour, Covent Garden, the market was devoted to the sale of fruit and vegetables, and offered a decided advantage to growers on account of its immediate proximity to the river, thus abolishing the porterage charges on goods which were consigned to Covent Garden by way of the Thames. In the seventeenth and eighteenth centuries, the roads, not only in the country, but even in London, were in such a neglected condition as to be almost impassable to wagon bearing loads of a perishable nature, such as fruits and vegetables, which necessitated a quick journey to the markets. The river, therefore, was a decidedly easier mode of transport, besides which some of the market-gardens were situated on the river bank. The most important of these were at Chelsea and were named the Neat-Houses. Strype describes them as "a parcel of Houses, most seated by the banks of the River Thames and inhabited by Gardiners; for which it is of note, for the supplying London and Westminster Markets with asparagus, artichokes, cauliflowers, musmelons, and the like useful things that the Earth produceth, which, by reason of their keeping the Ground so rich by dunging it (and through the nearness to London, they have the soil cheap), doth make their crops very forward, to their great Profit in coming to such good Markets." There were also Neat-Houses at Limehouse in Strype's time.

Hungerford market was not a success, and the fruit trade gradually deserted it, and in 1815 there were only about half a dozen butchers left in the market. It was rebuilt by Mr Charles Fowler, the same architect who rebuilt Covent Garden, in 1830, and was re-opened in 1833. Misfortune again pursued it, and it fell into a state of decay. The site is now occupied by Charing Cross Railway Station.

Portman Market was established in 1830 in the parish of Marylebone, but is heard of no more; and Clare Market is but a memory of the past. The present Borough, Spitalfields, and Stratford Markets are chiefly devoted to the sale of vegetables, and a very large proportion of the fruit sold there is drawn from Covent Garden or by growers who dispose of their own produce themselves.

The building of Covent Garden Market as we see it to-day dates back from 1829–30. The Act for the rebuilding was obtained by the sixth Duke of Bedford in 1827, who immediately had cleared away the miscellaneous ramshackle collection of stalls and sheds, the upper parts of which were inhabited by bakers, cooks, and retailers of gin, "to the detriment of the fair trader," who petitioned the Duke to rid the market of their apparently undesirable neighbours.

The present buildings consist of a central avenue of shops and rows facing north, south, east, and west, and intersected in the middle by a thoroughfare at right angles. The large spaces between the central avenue and the north and south rows are known as the "Apple" and

"Long" Markets respectively. The portion of the market situated between the Floral Hall Yard and Russell Street was erected about 1890, when the remaining portion of the eastern Piazza and the old Bedford Hotel were pulled down. It was known as the "Synagogue," probably on account of the number of salesmen of the Jewish persuasion who occupied stands there. A costermonger once summoned a salesman from this part of the market, and on being asked in court where he purchased the fruit in question, informed the judge, "In the Synagogue." "What?" said the judge. "Do you seriously mean to tell me that you purchased fruit in a place of worship?" It was then explained to his Lordship that the plaintiff referred to that portion of the market that was so nicknamed.

The "Jubilee" market is situated to the north of Tavistock Street and extends as far west as Southampton Street. It was so named on account of its erection in the year of Queen Victoria's Jubilee.

Covent Garden Market for many years after the rebuilding had a very insanitary reputation. It was christened "Mud Salad Market" by "Punch" because of the heaps of decayed vegetable matter which were allowed to accumulate within its precincts. It was supplied with water obtained from an artesian well situated under the middle of the central avenue. The water was pumped into cisterns placed under the roof covering the "Row." To-day, however, it is one of the best, if not *the* best kept market in the world.

It has been said that a pond existed in the middle of the square many years previous to the estate coming into the hands of the Bedford family. Its waters, fed by a spring, gained access to the Thames by way of Ivy Bridge Lane, where the Hotel Cecil is now. I have not been able to authenticate this fact, although quite recently, when the present premises of Messrs. T. Rochford and Geo. Monro, Ltd., were in course of erection in Tavistock Street, the construction of the foundations was seriously hampered by an inrush of water which necessitated pumps being kept at work for a considerable time. The presence of such a volume of water was attributed by the builder, I believe, to the improvements in Aldwych and Kingsway, which must have diverted some underground stream from its natural course.

The stone pavilions on the west side of the market were for many years tenanted by two dealers in herbs, only one of whom remains in the market, in the south-west corner. That in the north-west is now occupied by Mr J.B. Wright. The pavilion in the south-east corner was a coffee house named the "Carpenter's Arms," afterwards "Way's." Carpenter was formerly a market porter, and enjoyed some considerable renown on account of his ability to carry on his head fifteen half-bushel baskets of cherries from the wharf near that old-fashioned but now vanished tavern, the Fox-under-the-Hill by the Adelphi Arches. He could, in addition, throw off from the stack on his head from one to any number of baskets and never miss. The grower who chanced to see his fruit thus handled could not fail to be impressed by such a feat! According to Macmichael, he afterwards became lessee of the market.

"Way's" was the coffee-house mentioned by Dickens in "The Uncommercial Traveller", and was the scene of the meat pudding episode. "There was an early coffee to be got about Covent Garden Market, and that was more company—warm company, too, which was better. Toast of a very substantial quality was likewise procurable: though the touzled-headed man who made it, in an inner chamber within the coffee-room, hadn't got his coat on yet, and was so heavy with sleep that in every interval of toast and coffee he went off anew behind the partition into complicated cross-roads of choke and snore, and lost his way directly. Into one of these establishments (amongst the earliest) near Bow Street, there came one morning as I sat over my houseless cup, pondering where to go next, a man in a high and long snuff-coloured coat, and shoes, and, to the best of my belief, nothing else but a hat, who took out of his hat a large cold meat pudding; a meat pudding so large that it was a very tight fit and brought the lining out of the hat with it. This mysterious man was known by his pudding, for on his entering, the man of sleep brought him a pint of hot tea, a small loaf, and a large knife and fork and plate. Left to himself in his box, he stood the pudding on the bare table, and instead of cutting it, stabbed it, overhand, with the knife, like a mortal enemy; then took the knife out, wiped it on his sleeve, tore the pudding asunder with his fingers and eat it all up. The remembrance of this man with the pudding remains with me as the remembrance of the most spectral person my houselessness encountered. Twice only was I in that establishment, and twice I saw him stalk in (as I should say, just out of bed, and presently going back to bed), take out his pudding, stab his pudding, wipe the dagger, and eat his pudding all up. He was a man whose figure promised cadaverousness, but who had an excessively red face, though shaped like a horse's. On the second occasion of my seeing him, he said huskily to the man of sleep, 'Am I red to-night?' 'You are,' he uncompromisingly answered. 'My mother,' said the spectre, 'was a red-faced woman that liked drink, and I looked at her hard when she laid in her coffin, and I took the complexion.' Somehow the pudding seemed an unwholesome pudding after that and I put myself in his way no more."

The great novelist was a lover of the market and its busy scenes. In his early days, he says, "When I had nothing to do, I used to go to Covent Garden and stare at the pineapples."

"Covent Garden Market, when it was market morning, was wonderful company. The great wagons of cabbages, with growers, men, and boys lying asleep under them and with sharp dogs from market-garden neighbourhoods looking after the whole, was as good as a party. But one of the worst night-sights I know of in London is to be found in the children who prowl about this place; who sleep in the baskets, fight for the offal, dart at any objects they think they can lay their thieving hands on, dive under the carts and barrows, dodge the constables, and are perpetually making a blunt pattering on the pavement of the Piazza with the rain of their naked feet. A painful and unnatural result comes of the comparison one is forced to institute between the growth of corruption as displayed in the so much improved and cared-for fruits of the earth, and the growth of corruption as displayed in these uncared-for (except inasmuch as ever-hunted) savages."

"Way's" is now occupied by Messrs. H.T. Wooderson & Sons. Two other taverns were situated in the south row. The Green Dragon was in the middle and the White Horse, the last to disappear, was where Messrs. A. Israel & Sons are now. An old public-house named Salter's, which stood on the north-west corner of Russell Street, has also vanished, and there are no longer any taverns in Covent Garden Market proper. The upper parts of the present market shops were once the places of residence of their respective tenants. There are some alive to-day and who are connected with the market who were born in these minute chambers. It is not so very many years ago that the last person to reside in the market died in one of the rooms, which necessitated the lowering of the coffin out of the window like a safe, as it could not be brought downstairs on account of the premises having a spiral staircase.

Boswell relates how, "one night, when Beauclerk and Langton had supped at a tavern in London, and sat up till about three in the morning, it came into their heads to go and knock up Johnson, and see if they could prevail on him to join them in a ramble. They rapped violently at the doors of his chambers in the Temple, till at last he appeared in his shirt, with his little black wig on the top of his head instead of a night-cap, and, a poker in his hand, imagining, probably, that some ruffians were coming to attack him. When he discovered who they were, and was told their errand, he smiled, and with great good-humour agreed to their proposal. 'What, is it you, you dogs! I'll have a frisk with you.'

"He was soon dressed, and they sallied forth together into Covent Garden, where the greengrocers and fruiterers were beginning to arrange their hampers, just come in from the country. Johnson made some attempts to help them, but the honest gardeners stared so at his figure and manner, and odd interference, that he soon saw his services were not relished. They then repaired to one of the neighbouring taverns and made a bowl of that liquor called 'Bishop,' which Johnson had always liked" (Boswell's "Life of Johnson").

The pavilion facing the west entrance to the Floral Hall, and over which are the offices of the superintendent of the market and his staff, has for many years been tenanted by the Isaacs family, celebrated for the apparently inexhaustible supply of nuts of every description. The father of the present tenants was a humorous but very dry old gentleman, and was celebrated for his quaint sayings. He was sitting one afternoon in his shop after the day's business was over, smoking his church-warden pipe, when he was accosted by a smartly dressed gentleman who said that he had been informed that Mr Isaacs was a great authority on silkworms, and he would be greatly obliged if Mr Isaacs would be kind enough to inform him the best thing to give them for food. The old gentleman, thinking that he was being "got at," considered for a moment or so, then taking his pipe from between his teeth, said with great deliberation: "You see that street over there?" (pointing to James Street). "At the top of that street and round the corner you'll find a butcher's shop. Go inside and buy a pound of the best quality rump steak. Come back to the market and buy some new peas and new potatoes. Take 'em home and cook 'em and give 'em to the silkworms, and if the beggars won't eat that, they deserve to starve!"

There was a neighbour of his who had not the advantage of a very liberal education and who on being asked his opinion about the quality of a certain lot of lemons, signified his disapproval by saying, "Do you call those lemons? Why, if they had them in Liverpool, they'd throw 'em in the Thames!" He meant to say that the Liverpool dealers would consider the fruit as very common quality.

Yes! life in the market in the "good old days" was different from the struggle resulting from such keen competition of the present time. There are many who remember the days when the Centre Avenue or Grand Row was the fashionable promenade of an afternoon, filled with an everlasting crowd of elegant loungers who frittered away the time 'twixt scandal and flirtation, and the occasional interval for the purchase of a such an expensive item as a pineapple or a bundle of asparagus—when the outlying yards were filled with their splendid carriages and gorgeous flunkeys, and when Tavistock Street was quite as luxurious as the Regent Street of to-day. Such items as pines, asparagus, grapes, etc., were considered great luxuries, and commonly sold at such prices which if ever mentioned in the presence of a grower invariably draws from him the remark that "the trade is going to the dogs!" I know a certain grower of grapes who remembers the time when his father obtained 25s. and 30s. per lb. *wholesale* for his fruit!

The Grand Row is of course still in existence, with its magnificent displays of fruits and flowers. Can better blooms be found than at Phil Garcia? Those in search of the choicest fruits cannot do better than pay a visit to the shops of Mr Lewis Solomons (now Solomons & Chanter) who for many years have held the Royal Warrant, and have supplied fruit at some time or the other to almost every crowned head in Europe and I should think to everybody mentioned in Debrett.

Higher up the Row is "Barney." If he is not outside his shop he is certain to be found in the Floral Hall buying fresh stocks. His trade-mark is like Excelsior, "On a banner with a strange device—Barneyman." Other tenants of the Row are Miss Webber, Messrs. T.J. Poupart, Muxworthy, H. Rides, C. Kauffman, Beckett, J. Willis, Thomas Bros., Raines, and Garcia, Jacobs & Co. at the south-east corner. Overhead is the miniature "Zoo" known as the Bedford Conservatories, where goldfish, snakes, and other amphibians and birds are sold, and which is familiar to every visitor to the market. It used to be the favourite resort of the author wherein to regain his composure when as a little boy he had had the doubtful pleasure of interviewing a dentist!

The premises of Messrs. George Monro, Ltd., have already been described as being at both eastern corners of King Street and in the "Apple" Market.

But there are many important firms in the market besides those already mentioned. Mr Edward Isaacs under the Hummums Hotel, Messrs. Isaacs Bros. in James Street, where are also Messrs. Coupe & Son, Messrs. Margetson & Co. Ltd., Champion Bros., W. Dennis & Sons, Ltd., Messrs. Parsons & Co., who have also premises in the "Apple" Market, and Mr E.H. Lewis.

Messrs. Hazel & Steadman, Ltd., occupy the shop which was recently occupied by the hair-dressing saloon of the Tavistock Hotel. The present genial wielder of the razor, Fred, has been employed at the Tavistock for twenty-five years, and many a chin well known in sporting and Bohemian circles has claimed his attention. The first saloon used to be where the ground-floor dining-room is now. One day Fred was singeing the hair of a client when two street arabs happened to look in at the window, one of whom exclaimed, "Lumme, Bill, if there ain't a cove 'ere a-looking for 'em with a light!"

In the north row are the shops of Mr Rouse, Messrs. Vinden & Co., Messrs. L. Simmonds, Medlock, J. Thwaites, etc. In the east row are Messrs. John Lawrey, D. Kauffman, N. Nathan, S. Isaacs, George Wooderson, and Mack Bros. In the south are Messrs. George Coleman, T. Gibbs, T. Jay, etc. That genial sportsman "Uncle Dick" Foord has premises in the "Apple" Market, also Messrs. Edward Jacobs & Sons (and in the Floral Hall), Pankhurst & Co. and D.D. Pankhurst, H.G. Walker, H. Cherry, and Walter Frost. The chief tenants of the Long Market are Messrs. Staniforth & Whibley, W. Davis, J. Nathan, Major & Carr, Mr Pickering, etc.

Messrs. Ridley & Houlding and A. Jacobs & Sons are situated in Russell Street. Mr J. Emanuel occupies a shop at the corner of Wellington Street and Russell Street. Mr James Bradman, Messrs. Fenn & Hexton, Toole, B. Read & Co., Ltd., Mr Gerald da Costa, have premises in Floral Street.

The west side of the market is favoured with another humorist, Mike, who is supposed to be the salesman who fooled the costermonger about Hooper's Pharmacy as already related. Mike once summoned a customer for payment of his account who successfully pleaded, with the aid of copious tears, that he was unable to pay as he had invested all his takings in ginger beer, which owing to the heat of the weather, had all exploded in the night! On another occasion he paid a visit to a client who was behind in his payment, and the only satisfaction he was able to obtain was a solo on a tin whistle appropriately entitled "The Lost Chord."

The greatest character of all was without doubt "Uncle Teddy." The quaint sayings of this dear old gentleman would fill a volume. His chief place of business in later years was in the Floral Hall. He was for some time at open war with his next-door neighbour, who had entered into an unsuccessful speculation in onions, and the weather having turned warm and damp, the onions began to behave as this particular vegetable does under such conditions, to the great annoyance of "Uncle Teddy." One day a gentleman acquaintance happened to stroll through the market, and went up to him, saying, "Good morning, sir. How goes the enemy?" "Filled up with onions," came the instant reply. (The gentleman only meant to ask the time.)

On another occasion he was leaving his place of business in the Floral Hall when he overheard some of the porters swearing (a not at all unusual occurrence). The old gentleman immediately flew into a rage. "I'll lock you up! I'll put an end to this swearing," and beckoning an old servant who stood by, told him to fetch a policeman "to lock these men up for making use of bad language." The old servant, who was rather hard of hearing, did not hear what was said, and putting his hand up to hear, said, "What did you say, governor?" Teddy, forgetting what he had said and where he was for the moment, shouted at the old man, "Go on, you old fool, go and get a policeman!" The laughter of the crowd which had been attracted to the spot suddenly reminded him what he had just said. He never uttered another word, but, tucking his umbrella under his arm, he crept away to lunch.

One morning he arrived at business and casually remarked, "It won't rain to-day." Some buyer who stood by said that he thought it would. Immediately Teddy offered to bet anybody that it would not rain before midday, and then and there accepted bets from dozens of porters and buyers. About eleven o'clock the heavens became overcast and the work of the market began to be seriously inconvenienced by the porters every moment stopping work to look at the weather. At last, about ten minutes to twelve, a few drops of rain fell amidst such cheers that nearly brought the roof of the Floral Hall off, and brought crowds of people in from Bow Street and the market to see what the noise was about. That morning cost the old gentleman about fifty pounds.

I shall never forget the day when the French goods were late and he ran down to Waterloo Bridge to see if he could hurry up any van he might happen to meet. At last he found one heavily laden van crawling along, which after a deal of tipping he managed to get quickly up to the market. On calling on his men to unload, the carman quietly said, "This ain't your load, governor; it's for Garcia" (the opposite firm of Garcia, Jacobs & Co.).

His brother Sam was just the reverse. He was very quiet and retiring, and for years enjoyed the reputation of being known a "The Radish King," on account of his being the largest receiver of radishes in the United Kingdom. Both the brothers have now passed the bourne whence no traveller returns. Peace be to their ashes!

The Floral Hall is connected with one of the greatest practical jokes ever perpetrated in the market. A certain buyer, whom we will name here as Mr. X, went to a sale of miscellaneous property with a friend who was connected with one of the broker in the Floral Hall. This gentleman had occasion to purchase some pictures for his new house, and immediately after a certain picture had been knocked down to him, he was asked by a stranger if he would accept a profit for it. Mr X, who was of a very suspicious nature, promptly advised his friend not to sell it, saying that he thought the picture was a valuable one and at the same time claimed half-shares if it should turn out to be of any particular worth. The gentleman, who was disgusted at his friend's greed, determined to play a practical joke on him. He thereupon promised him half-shares, and the next day took one or two of his intimate friends into his confidence, with the result that the picture was presumably offered to a certain firm of Bond Street dealers who offered £1,500 and who eventually increased their offer to £4,000. The joke was so exceedingly well worked up that it was believed by everybody. Mr X purchased for his wife some valuable jewellery and furs, and in order to celebrate the occasion invited a few choice friends to a champagne luncheon at "Gow's" in the Strand. After a sumptuous repast, the party strolled in the direction of the market, and when at length they reached the Piazzas, a telegram was handed to the gentleman, who, after perusing its contents, pretended to faint. "What's the matter?" exclaimed Mr X, suddenly seized with the sense of impending disaster. "Read this," said one of his friends, putting the telegram into his hand, which was to the effect that the picture was a forgery and that the cheque was consequently stopped.

By this time the joke had become public property, and the next morning there was a great crowd in the Hall to witness the arrival of the "victim," who was greeted with loud cheers and a great amount of chaff. During the morning a rough sketch on a piece of paper was offered for sale from a neighbouring rostrum as a "Meissonier," which after a deal of good natured horse-play was knocked down to a costermonger for 50,000 guineas. It was some time before Mr X dared show his face in the market again.

Several years ago a large stack of empty baskets caught fire in one of the cellars under the Hall and caused great excitement in the neighbourhood, but without doing any serious damage to the Hall. In the midst of the confusion some of the market officials attempted to play on the flames by means of a hose of very small proportions which they fixed to a tap inside the Hall. Immediately the water was turned on, the official who held the hose dropped it like a hot coal, as did everybody who attempted to hold it. It was then discovered that the pipe which fed this particular tap passed through the cellar where the fire was raging, and consequently the water was boiling!

Messrs. E.A. O'Kelly, Edward Jacobs & Sons, W. Dennis & Sons, Ltd., J.B. Thomas, Woolf & Jacobs, and Garcia, Jacobs & Co. are the present tenants of the Floral Hall.

XIV

Conclusion

All varieties of fruit are to-day so plentiful that it is somewhat difficult to say which enjoys the greatest amount of popularity. The orange for over two centuries has been consumed in ever-increasing quantities. Both Pepys and Ben Jonson made frequent allusions to the orange-girls who retailed the luscious fruit to the theatre-going public, which proves that even in their time the orange was an important marketable commodity. It is said that Sir Walter Raleigh first imported the fruit into England.

What would Mistress Eleanor Gwynn say if she were able to revisit the scenes of her youth and behold the vast quantities of the golden fruit which are annually dealt with in London! Some idea of the magnitude of this traffic may be gained from the fact that the province of Valencia, in Spain, alone annually exports a total of about 4,000,000 cases to the United Kingdom, each case containing from 420 to 1,064 oranges, according to size. The seedless variety of such exceptional size and beauty is grown in that fruit-grower's paradise—California. It is also being cultivated on a smaller scale (at present) in Australia and South Africa, and even in India.

Apples are eaten in exceptionally large quantities in this country. The chief source of production is America. The dessert varieties are grown in California and Oregon, the Wenatchee Valley, and our own colonies of British Columbia and Nova Scotia. The cooking kinds come from Canada, New York State, Nova Scotia, and Maine and Virginia.

The crop of apples grown in Australia and Tasmania is a very large one, and is one of the most important branches of the fruit trade, and has increased to a remarkable degree within the last few years. The chief centres of apple production in the United Kingdom are Kent, Middlesex, Lincoln, Worcestershire, and Somersetshire, and also the north of Ireland. The best fruit is grown in the two first-mentioned counties; the immediate vicinity around Maidstone, known as the "Weald of Kent," is well noted for its fine quality fruit. The Kentish growers have, within the last three years, endeavoured to adopt a more uniform system of packing, consistent with that in vogue in the large apple-producing parts of America. Their endeavours, I am glad to say, have met with a considerable amount of success, although I must admit that this only applies to the dessert varieties (so far as the box packing is concerned). By this means it has been possible to export to such places as South American and South African ports, important quantities of British-grown apples, which have in the majority of cases arrived in good condition. The large "cookers" should be packed in barrels on the American plan, and the sooner the trees bearing inferior kinds of small fruit which are at present so extensively cultivated in this country are dug out of the ground, the better it will be for the English grower. The chief drawback he has had to contend with is the amount of useless timber with which his orchards are littered, and which, in a great many instances, he is unable to "grub out" through lack of capital. If the Government, through the Board of Agriculture, assisted farmers financially to improve their holdings, the growers in this country would be able to compete on better terms with those in other states.

Strawberries are grown in Hampshire and Kent, and also around Wisbech. The strawberry season is generally of such short duration that when the fruit is on the market, every other variety has to "play second fiddle." It is then that the trade suffers from that annual epidemic familiarly known to both grower and salesman as the "strawberry fever." The failure of the crop of strawberries is a grievous disappointment to the fruit-loving public. Lemons come from Italy and Spain. English cherries are grown principally in Kent, as are also gooseberries, raspberries, and plums. Some of the Midland counties, principally Worcestershire and Gloucestershire, grow important quantities of similar fruit which supply principally the northern and midland markets. Large quantities of pears, plums, greengages, and cherries come from France and reach London by way of the Thames by the Bennett Steamship Company, whose vessels are discharged just below London Bridge at Chamberlain's Wharf. There is also the direct service via Boulogne and Folkestone (S.E & C.R.), whose trains are unloaded at Bricklayers' Arms and Blackfriars Stations. Holland and Belgium also export important consignments of both fruit and vegetables. Indeed, Holland has for centuries been much in advance of this country in the cultivation of vegetables. John Noorthouck in his "History of London", mentions in his description of the metropolis in the reign of Henry VIII that "so little were vegetables cultivated, or gardening understood as yet, that in the year 1509 Queen Catherine could not procure a salad, until Henry sent to the Netherlands, and engaged a gardener to come over to raise the proper articles here."

The more expensive kinds of grapes, melons, peaches, tomatoes, and cucumbers are grown under glass. The knowledge and skill which are essential to a successful grower of any of these varieties is not suddenly acquired, but is the result of lifelong experience, and in the majority of instances is handed down from father to son. The diseases which affect every product grown under glass are as numerous and quite as deadly as those which attack the human frame, but, thanks to science, they are gradually being overcome. The Lea Valley, Essex, is the home of the glass-houses, which extend from Enfield nearly as far as Ware in Hertford. The most important growers are the Rochfords and the Hamiltons.

Guernsey also produces a vast quantity of flowers, grapes, tomatoes, and potatoes, also peas and beans. Worthing is a second Lea Valley.

The finest dessert apples and pears are grown in California. The largest exporters are the A. Block Fruit Company and the Earl Fruit Company. The pears handled by these firms are the grandest in the world, and consist of the William, Doyenne du Comic Beurre Hardy, Glout Morceau, Winter Nelis, and the Easter Beurre. The Producer's Fruit Company are also well known as shippers of excellent quality fruit.

The Flower Market is situated on the west side of Wellington Street, and extends as far back as the "Jubilee" Market, partly over which has recently been erected a new market for the sale of French flowers. The shops in Tavistock and York Streets are almost all occupied by flower salesmen.

No market would be complete without the costermonger, and Covent Garden is no exception to this rule. The word "costermonger" is an abbreviation of "costardmonger," who was originally a vendor of apples: hence his name. According to the old dramatists, many of the clan were sons of Erin and of none too sweet a temper.

> And then he'll rail like a rude costermonger
> That schoolboys have cozened of his apple
> As loud and senseless.
>
> (BEAUMONT AND FLETCHER)

The fruit trade generally is under a sense of deep obligation to these gentry, as without them the accumulations of an overstocked market in times of glut could never be disposed of.

Potatoes were sold in the streets as early as the reign of James I., and "Cherry Ripe" was a favourite of the seventeenth century.

No account of the market would be complete without mention of those growers who dispose of their own produce themselves. Foremost amongst them are Messrs. Lobjoint of Brentford, Walter Mann, A.W. Smith of Feltham, Messrs. J. & W. Edmonds, the Brothers Tile, Mr Bartholomews, etc.

One of the most celebrated market gardeners to make use of Covent Garden was Edmund Burke. On September 10, 1771, he wrote to Arthur Young "My carrots last year were remarkably fine. I sold as much as brought fourteen pounds and I am convinced that if I had known Covent Garden as I do now, I should have sold the same weight for near thirty" (Burke's Letters). It seems to have been quite as difficult to satisfy growers in those days as now.

The time to see Covent Garden at its busiest is on a summer morning between five and six o'clock. The vans of the fruiterers and greengrocers are arranged in the middle of the streets surrounding the market, to which the porters are busily engaged in carrying the recently purchased goods. The market itself is crowded by a heterogeneous collection of humanity. Here and there amongst the crowd of buyers are to be seen a couple of nuns in their sombre garments; whilst a few sweet-faced nurses in uniform, with bunches of flowers under their arms wherewith to refresh the wards in the great hospitals, add a splash of colour to the animated scene. At nine o'clock there is a lull, when both buyers and salesmen adjourn to breakfast at the Tavistock, the Hummums, or the Bedford Head. The vans have by now all disappeared, bearing their stocks to shops as far north as Finchley, and Woolwich in the east, Kew and Richmond in the west, and Croydon in the south.

At ten o'clock the auction sales commence in the Floral Hall, and by this time the crowd is augmented by buyers from all over the country. About midday the Hall belches forth its vast quantities to the waiting railway and to the salesmen's shops in the market and neighbourhood, and as the afternoon progresses, the market gradually quietens down as it were to a well-earned rest until the evening, when the country carts and motor-lorries again appear, bringing their never-ending supplies for the next day's market. Mr W.S. Landor tersely summed up the history of Covent Garden in the following lines:

"The convent becomes a playhouse monks and nuns turn actors and actresses. The garden, formal and quiet, where a salad was cut for a lady abbess and flowers were gathered to adorn images, becomes a market, noisy and full of life, distributing thousands of packages of fruit and flowers to a vicious metropolis."

Appendix

The derivation of the name Covent Garden has been frequently discussed, especially among the old historians of London. It appears to be the consensus of opinion that Covent Garden was originally the garden belonging to the monastery at Westminster; yet Strype, in his revision of Stow's "History of London", distinctly states: "It hath probably the name Covent Garden because it was the garden and fields to that large monastery or convent where Exeter House stood; these grounds belonging unto it, being all encompassed with a wall, and when this ground upon the Dissolution of the Religious Houses became the estate of his Grace's ancestors, then Bedford House was erected where it now stands, or lately did, whereas before this house was on the other side of the Strand, called the Bishop of Carlisle's Inn."

Strype is at fault, because he confuses the Exeter House of the Lord Burleigh with a noble mansion of the same name which stood in the Outer Temple. In Maitland's "London" vol. ii. p. 1336, I find: "At the Dissolution of the Order of the Knights Templars, the advowson of this church [St Clement Danes], together with lands and five messuages in the parish, were conferred upon the Prior and Canons Regular of the Church of the Holy Sepulchre, which lands and messuages, I imagine, will appear to have been that part of the Temple called the Outer. For in the year 1324, the said Prior and Canons having disposed of the same to Walter, Bishop of Exeter, he erected thereon a stately edifice, or a City Mansion, for himself and his successors, and denominated the same, Exeter House. This Fabric, being some time after alienated, it came to the noble families of Paget and Leicester, and at last to that of Essex, and being since, pulled down, a beautiful street (the present Essex Street) is erected on the site thereof by the appellation of the last noble possessor."

No monastery ever occupied the site of Lord Burleigh's house, but the Exeter House which Strype refers to was erected in 1324 on lands belonging to the Church.

Hart Street.—Mr Cunningham, in his "Handbook of London", states that this street was named after an inn called the White Hart, mentioned in the Cecil lease of September 1570 already referred to in this book; but as the White Hart is described in the lease which appears in "Archæologia", vol. xxx. p. 494, as being situated in the Strand, it is by no means clear that it is after this particular inn that the street was named. There was also a White Hart at the north-east end of Drury Lane, at the corner of High Street, St Giles, which was of some antiquity. A public-house of this name still exists, but has recently been quite rebuilt.

Covent Garden did not escape the ravages of the Great Plague, for Pepys noted on July 6, 1665: "I could not see Lord Brouncker, nor had much mind, one of the great houses within two doors of him in Covent Garden being shut up, and Lord! the number of houses visited and which this day I observed through the town, quite round in my way by Long Lane and London Wall."

James Street.—A public-house named the Nagg's Head stood here in the time of Strype. That part of the street between this place of refreshment and Long Acre was not nearly so well inhabited as the portion towards the market.

Strype gives the inward boundaries of the parish of St Paul, Covent Garden, as follows: "I shall begin on the west side of the Duke of Bedford's House next the Strand where it crosseth into Maiden Lane and runneth on the Backside of the houses into Halfmoon Street, taking in both sides of this Lane: And from the Halfmoon Street it also runneth on the Backside of Shandois Street, on the south side unto the Tallow-chandler's, which is a little beyond Round Court, where it crosseth the street, as also the houses betwixt Bedford Bury and Bedford Court, and so into New Street, which it crosseth, and runs down the Backside of White Rose Street, next to James Street, and Talleth into Red Rose Street, where it crosseth the houses and falleth into Hart Street, on the Backside of the buildings next Long Acre, taking in part of James Street, by the Nagg's Head Inn; and so along the Backside of Hart Street unto the corner of Bow Street: And there it crosseth into Red Lion Court, taking in all the houses except two or three next Bow Street; and so along the Backside of Bow Street into Russel Street, two doors from the Rose Tavern; and thence crosseth the houses on the east side of Brydges Street, and falls into the West End of White Hart Yard where it crosseth into Exeter Street and runneth along unto Bedford back wall, taking in the south side as aforesaid; and at the Wall runs down the West Side of Curle Court into the Strand, and so to the Duke of Bedford's House where I began the inward bounds."

Bow Street.—This street did not at one time run into Long Acre. The only means of access to it from the north was by way of Broad Court or by Red Lion Court from Drury Lane. This court was situated on the east side between Long Acre and Broad Court, and has now disappeared.

"The growth of London has pushed the market-gardener gradually into the country, and now, instead of sending up his produce by his own wagons, he trusts it to the railways and is often thrown into a market fever by a late delivery. To compensate him, however, for the altered state of the times, he often sells his crops like a merchant upon 'Change, without the trouble of bringing more than a few hand samples in his pockets. He is nearly seventy years of age but looks scarcely fifty, and can remember the time when there were ten thousand acres of ground within four miles of Charing Cross under cultivation for vegetables, besides about three thousand acres planted with fruit to supply the London consumption. He has lived to see the Deptford and Bermondsey gardens curtailed; the Hoxton and Hackney gardens covered with houses; the Essex plantations pushed farther off; and the Brompton and Kensington nurseries—the home of vegetables for centuries—dug up and sown with International Exhibition temples and Italian gardens that will never grow a pea or send a single cauliflower to market. He has lived to see Guernsey and Jersey, Cornwall, the Scilly Islands, Holland, Belgium, and Portugal, with many other more distant places, competing with the remote outskirts of London bricks and mortar, and has been staggered by seeing the market supplied with choice early peas from such an unexpected quarter as French Algeria" ("Cornhill Magazine," 1866).

As will be seen from the above, London was renowned for its gardens. This fact was recorded as early as the reign of Henry II (1154–1189) by FitzStephen. The royal garden at Westminster was noted for its magnificent blooms in 1276. Stow noted that "Within the compass of one age, Somerset House and the buildings were called country-houses; and the open places about them were employed in gardens for profit; and also many parts within the City and liberties were occupied by working gardeners and were sufficient to furnish the town with garden-ware; for then but a few herbs were used at the table as compared to what are spent now."

Holborn (Oldbourne) was celebrated for its gardens, especially those belonging to Ely House:

> DUKE OF GLOU.:
> My Lord of Ely, when I was last in Holborn
> I saw good strawberries in your garden there;
> I do beseech you send for some of them.
>   B. OF ELY: Marry, and will, my lord, with all my heart.
>   ("Richard III," Act iii. sc. 4)

The site of Lincoln's Inn Fields was for years renowned for the fine fruit grown there. The accounts of the bailiff, when the garden supplied Lincoln House, mention that apples, pears, large nuts and cherries, sufficient for the Earl of Lincoln's use, and what was over yielded in one year £135 modern currency (Timbs). Clerkenwell also produced a fair quantity of vegetables, and the site of Buckingham Palace (Goring House) boasted a cherry-garden and also a kitchen-garden. Wailer described the wall in St James's Park as "all with a border of rich fruit-trees crown'd."

In 1828 the site of Trinity Church, Brompton, was a large market garden. In South Lambeth was a celebrated garden which existed in 1749 and belonged to Tradescant, the "King's Gardener." Besides many varieties of flowers, pappas, or Virginian potatoes, fox grapes from Virginia, white and red Burlett grapes, currant grapes, "Muscadells," "Frontinack or Musked grapes, white and red," British Queen strawberries, and "Hippomarathrum" or rhubarb of the monks were cultivated here.

There were also other gardens, both in and around the metropolis, where herbs and medicinal roots were largely grown.

Belton Street. This street was at one time named Hanover Street, A public-house stood here which was advertised as "A Handsome Corner Public-house, in New Belton-Street, St Giles ... just empty, well situated and free from the Bondage of any particular Brewer." This advertisement appeared in "The Daily Courant" of December 27, 1726, to be let on lease, and is noteworthy as being an exceedingly early example of the working of the tied-house system affecting licensed premises ("Notes and Queries", 11, s. vii. January 4, 1913).

Also available from Nonsuch Publishing

Alexander, Boyd (ed.)	*The Journal of William Beckford in Portugal and Spain*	978 1 84588 010 1
Brontë, Rev. Patrick	*The Letters of the Rev. Patrick Brontë*	978 1 84588 066 8
Broughton, S.D.	*Letters from Portugal, Spain and France*	978 1 84588 030 9
Brunel, Isambard	*The Life of Isambard Kingdom Brunel, Civil Engineer*	978 1 84588 031 6
Coleman, E.C. (ed.)	*The Travels of Sir John Mandeville, 1322–1356*	978 184588 075 0
Corbett, Sir Julian	*The Campaign of Trafalgar*	978 1 84588 059 0
Duff, Charles	*A Handbook on Hanging*	978 1 84588 141 2
Eyre, Lt Vincent	*The Military Operations at Cabul*	978 1 84588 012 5
Fothergill, A. Brian	*Beckford of Fonthill*	978 1 84588 085 9
Fothergill, A. Brian	*Sir William Hamilton: Envoy Extraordinary*	978 1 84588 042 2
Gooch, Sir Daniel	*The Diaries of Sir Daniel Gooch*	978 1 84588 016 3
Greenwood, Lt John	*The Campaign in Afghanistan*	978 1 84588 004 0
Hammond, J.L. and Barbara	*The Village Labourer*	978 1 84588 056 9
Hawkes, Francis L.	*Commodore Perry and the Opening of Japan*	978 1 84588 026 2
Helps, Sir Arthur	*The Life and Labours of Thomas Brassey*	978 1 84588 011 8
Hill, Wg Cdr Roderic	*The Baghdad Air Mail*	978 1 84588 009 5
Hudson, W.H.	*Idle Days in Patagonia*	978 1 84588 024 8
Jefferies, Richard	*Wildlife in a Southern County*	978 1 84588 064 4
Livingstone, David and Charles	*Expedition to the Zambesi and its Tributaries*	978 1 84588 065 1
Matthews, Henry	*Diary of an Invalid*	978 1 84588 017 0
Park, Mungo	*Travels in the Interior of Africa*	978 1 84588 068 2
Scott, Capt. Robert F.	*The Voyage of the Discovery, Vol. One*	978 1 84588 057 6
Ségur, Gen. Count Philippe de	*Memoirs of an Aide de Camp of Napoleon, 1800–1812*	978 1 84588 005 7
Simmonds, P.L.	*Sir John Franklin and the Arctic Regions*	978 1 84588 007 1

For forthcoming titles and sales information see

www.nonsuch-publishing.com